MW00653920

Contents

Introduction

It was an autumn afternoon in September, 2005. The sanctuary was peaceful and the sunbeams cast a powerful glow through the beautiful stained glass windows that adorned the walls of the old cathedral. From the main floor of the church, the pastor invited members of the congregation to share some words with their fellow churchgoers. A grey-haired woman, somewhat bent over and walking with a peculiar gait, made her way to the front of the sanctuary. As she came alongside the pastor, he smiled and motioned for her to speak.

The woman turned to face the people who waited, and she said, "It is very important that you get into the word. You need to spend time in the word in order to come to know our God. He is ready to speak to you when you spend time in the word."

The woman hesitated, then continued, "Our God is very faithful to those who come to Him. He desires to bless you and work wonders in your life. All He asks is that you come to know Him and spend time with Him."

I listened to the voice of this elderly soul and felt like God was speaking directly to me. Considering her age, I thought her voice was strong, but her message was even more powerful. It was clear to me that this was a person who walked with the Lord.

In closing, the woman shared stories about her work in Africa, and told the people about the miracles that God had done in her life.

"I was very sick for most of my life," she said. "Now, at 80 years of age, God has continued to bless me in countless ways."

I was struck by the presence of this woman in the sanctuary. She held the attention of the people and one knew that her words came from a genuine heart. My thoughts were interrupted as the pastor asked others to come forward. The woman returned to her seat. It was obvious mobility was difficult for her.

A few others made their way to the front of the church that September afternoon and shared stories about their lives, but it was that woman's story that resonated with my heart. The tales told by the others have been forgotten but her message has remained.

The pastor invited the congregation to meet in the lower hall following the service. He announced that the church was providing soup and a bun for those who would like to share a meal and a time of fellowship. The church was located in the inner city, so the meal was part of its outreach into the community. I was new to the church, but I decided I would join the others in the lower hall. I stood and made my way down the stairs where I found a long line of people waiting to receive their food.

I received my portion and I looked about the large room for a place to eat my meal. I walked down one row of tables, and there before my eyes, sat the elderly woman who had spoken in the sanctuary just moments before. I asked if I could sit beside her and she moved over to make room for me.

That was where our story began—in an inner city church on a September afternoon. I was introduced to an elderly woman who has affected my life with her love of God.

6

Following my introduction to Helena Peters, I was invited to join her in her outreach ministry. We travelled to various drop-in centres around the City of Winnipeg. I was witness to her loving and caring way with people from the inner city, who were living such impoverished lives. She sang hymns and songs while she played her omni-chord. She talked to them about the gospel, asked questions, and showed a genuine interest in their lives. Most of all, when she left their presence, in prayer, she took their needs with her to her heavenly father.

Helena and I attended church together in a number of chapels throughout the city. We talked at length over the phone and made plans to visit with each other. We shared special times of prayer in the Prayer Furnace, and at meetings of the End time Handmaidens and Servants. We attended mission conferences and the Franklin Graham Revival. She introduced me to the Billy Graham Telephone Ministry and to countless other resources for the benefit of my spiritual walk with the Lord. It has been a blessing from the Lord that I have been able to spend time and fellowship with her. I have stayed with her in her home and have observed her ways over the course of time.

Helena shared stories of her life with me. It has been an honour and a privilege to hear about her trips to Africa and to appreciate her tireless efforts to support children in the feeding centres and the orphanage she founded in Nairobi, Kenya.

When Helena Peters disembarked onto the shore of Newfoundland as a young girl, her whole life was unknown to her. In fact, it was as foreign as the land on which she stood. Her life was a blank canvas but God had mapped out a journey for her to follow. It was a narrow path that reached far into the depths of the hearts of people.

Helena provides comfort and encouragement to all those who cross her path. She demonstrates the courage spoken of in the Bible: courage to persevere, courage to overcome, and courage to be triumphant over aches and pains, fatigue and mental challenges.

Helena chooses to present herself with a positive and upbeat countenance. When she phones me to share the activities of her day, her first words are full of life and enthusiasm. On greeting, she says, "Hi there!" with a voice that carries a special lilt that makes me feel like she is so happy to see me and speak with me.

The fullness and energy expressed in her mannerisms, Helena attributes to the Lord. She explains that it is the resurrection power that is given to those who have chosen to follow Jesus that keeps her moving and singing and giving to others.

When asked how she is doing, Helena often replies, "Well. I'm fine! The Lord has blessed me with this and the Lord has blessed me with that. Praise God. He has done this for me and He has done that for me." She is continually singing His praises and honouring Him with her attitude of gratitude.

Helena's selfless pursuits keep her attentive to the needs of those around her. Her home is a beehive of activity. Moments at home are few, but when she is in her own space you can hear the commotion of busy hands and the sound of Christian music, which permeates her environment. She allows the words and music to flood her heart and mind and keep her flowing in the spirit.

She spends a great deal of time making booklets and other resources to give to others. Her booklets are comprised of songs, verses, poems and artwork that she has received from the Lord. She shares her gifts openly and freely with others. Banners that are the handiwork of Helena Peters are displayed in churches in the City of Winnipeg, in Mexico, Nicaragua, Maui, Hawaii, and in Africa. They carry a message of hope and encouragement. One reads: "Jesus gave His life for me in love. I will never be truly happy until, in love, I give my all to Him."

In the world today, people concern themselves with items being sold out when they reach the store. They focus on the here and now. In contrast, Helena Peters focuses on the eternal. She is "sold out" for God.

Conversations with Helena have been encouraging and inspirational. She has demonstrated an inspired life, remaining focused on her life goal: to share the gospel to the ends of the earth. She has travelled to remote places and to busy, congested cities. She has felt led by the Lord to many different countries and a number of continents.

No matter where God takes her, Helena rests in the knowledge that the Lord walks with her. In that blessed assurance, she remains His willing and obedient servant.

In the world today, people talk about how to carve out more time for themselves from their very busy schedules. Helena keeps a schedule that many individuals decades younger than her would have a difficult time maintaining. In this world, people live by the words of William Shakespeare: "To thine own self be true." In contrast, Helena looks to the Lord for direction and guidance. She lives by the words, "Oh Lord, not my will, but your will be done."

Helena walks her talk. She moves through her moments heeding the words of the gospel as spoken by Jesus. Her single-minded focus has not always gained her acceptance in all circles, but she has been secure in knowing that what she does is of eternal significance. She walks on with hope in her heart because, daily, she spends time in the word and even more time in prayer.

Often times, Helena will say to me, "We have to really pray for ..."

I like to think of Helena as a prayer warrior. I have been witness to her prayer watch, which often begins at four in the morning and continues through the day until sometime around ten at night. Many nights have been spent in prayer at the expense of her own rest. Helena rests in the Lord.

On many occasions, I would suggest to Helena that someone should write about her walk with God and, to my surprise, one day she turned to me and said, "I want you to write my story."

I hope you enjoy and are inspired by the spiritual journey of Helena Peters. I encourage you to read the comments shared by others who have journeyed alongside Helena. Thank you to all of those individuals who were willing to reveal their experience with this woman of God.

Valerie Minaker

Helena's Story

One

In the Beginning

Long before I was born, our family roots dated back to Holland. My ancestors were forced to leave Holland during the persecution. Reportedly, people were required to take a pledge not to proselyte. Individuals who refused to take the pledge were sent to South America. It was very difficult to earn a living in South America and the people endured long days of hard labour. My ancestors opted to move to the Ukraine. The Mennonite Central Committee provided assistance to my family and made the arrangements for their emigration to the new land.

It was very taxing on those people who opted not to proselyte. Individuals felt great guilt because not being able to share their faith was contrary to the tenets of their religion. My father was helpless in this situation because his own parents were well settled in the Ukraine at the time of his birth. He was consumed with guilt for most of his life.

My parents, David and Agnes Dyck, (nee Kroeker), were married and made their home in the Ukraine. They welcomed me as their first child on March 11, 1925. They named me Helena Dyck, after my maternal grandmother. Later, our family grew to include brothers and sisters.

My father was a farmer, a teacher, and a minister. Farming provided food for the table. I remember a large vegetable garden and many fruit trees on our property. The communist gangs came and demanded various things from us and stole our food. Basically, they left the residents of the village to starve to death. My mother breast-fed me but, due to nutritional deficiencies, her milk was like water. When I was taken for medical attention my body was limp. The doctor told my father that I was almost dead. As a result of poor nutrition, I had developed rickets.

The communist gangs ordered individual farmers to drive them to the next village. Each farmer was required to use his own wagon. The communists tracked the farmers by referring to a list. My grandfather knew that my father was going to be called next and took my father aside and explained.

"My children are fully grown but your children are still so young. I will take your place when they come to have you drive your wagon."

A short time later, my grandfather went with the communists. He was never seen again. In my eyes, my grandfather was a great man to do what he did for us. He sacrificed his life for ours, and I was robbed of the opportunity to know him.

My mother was a very kind woman. She extended kindness to the Russians as well. One time, my throat was so swollen that it was closing my airway. A Russian woman came to our house and instructed my mother to add a bit of vinegar to water. With this solution on a cloth, my mother was guided to reach in and wash my throat. The solution was heaven-sent. My breathing was restored.

God was watching over me when he sent that Russian woman to our home.

"When a man's ways please the LORD, *He maketh even his enemies to be at peace with him"* (Proverbs 16:7).

When the communist regime gathered strength, my father was ordered to stop teaching. The communists were not pleased with his way of teaching because he was a Christian. As a result, his name was put on a blacklist.

My family wanted to escape the fear and oppression weighing on the people in the Ukraine. People feared they would be sent to Siberia. My father was not content to sit and wait so he planned our escape. He knew that in order for his plan to be successful, he would have to provide a bribe to the top officials. He killed a cow and butchered it into four pieces. Each top official received one quarter.

There hath no temptation taken you but such as is common to man: but God is faithful, who will not suffer you to be tempted, above that ye are able: but will with the temptation also make a way to escape, that ye may be able to bear it (1 Corinthians 10:13).

On a bright, sunny day in the fall of 1929, some of the women from our church in Milaradofka, Ukraine, took a group of innocent children to the woods for a day of frolicking. We looked at the many brightly coloured leaves on the trees and marveled at the beauty of nature. Following such a wonderful afternoon, I was excited to return home and tell my family all about our adventures in the forest.

I got to our house and opened the door that led to the kitchen. It was dark inside! My uncle was there in the darkness. He silenced me.

"Be quiet," he whispered. "All are sleeping... You are going on a long trip tonight so you are to go to bed now."

I was puzzled and disappointed that I could not share my excitement with anyone. I had to go to sleep? What was happening?

Later that night, when all was dark outside, we were put in a horse-drawn wagon. We were going to travel, but why? In my mind, I questioned what was happening. The houses in the village remained in darkness. Concerned that someone would notice our movements, the fear welled up inside of me. We had left everything behind except some food and clothing. I was afraid of the dark. Was someone lurking there in the shadows? Fearful thoughts kept racing through my mind. I felt myself shivering in the night. Finally, I asked my father, "Why are we travelling?

"You won't understand now," he answered. "One day you will understand my child… They want to send me to Siberia and we would all starve to death there."

"Yesterday, we had so much fun in the woods!" I said. My voice carried excitement but I knew that he did not hear me. Then he tried to reassure me.

"Trust me," he said. "I know what is best for us. We must pray that the communists do not get us. We must pray that we get to Canada safely."

I was angry with my father for taking me from what I felt was a happy and nice place. Why couldn't I tell anyone about the fun I had had the day before? Why? I was scared. I was four and a half years old.

Many times since that trip long ago, I have thought about how thankful I am for my father bringing us to Canada. As a child, I could not understand what was happening. But my father was right when he said, "Someday you will understand."

God protected us and we arrived in Canada the following spring. That childhood experience reminds me to trust my heavenly Father, who knows what is ahead. As a child of God, I need to trust my loving Father, God. Yes, Father knows best!

"For as the heavens are higher than the earth, so are my ways higher than your ways, and my thoughts than your thoughts" (Isaiah 55:9).

From the wagon, we boarded a train headed for Moscow. We had to be diligent about concealing our identity, which was

especially true for my father. We were told to be quiet, to make
no noise, and to draw no attention to ourselves. My father was
uncertain whether we would reach Moscow before the officials
would learn of his departure.

Upon arrival in Moscow, my father immediately went to the
Russian Embassy. He needed to secure permission to leave the
country. We had to wait a couple of days before the paperwork
would be completed. During that time, we visited a building that
housed an aquarium. I was enchanted by dolphins playing in the
water. They came near to me and I responded as any child
would, with joy and excitement in my voice. People were watching my enthusiasm with interest and when my father noticed, he
sternly, but quietly, redirected me away from the dolphins.

"We have to stay together," he said. "We cannot risk having
anyone see me. Come with me now," he urged.

Father finally collected the necessary papers and we left
Moscow, travelling by train to Germany. Still, we could not let
our guard down. We had to remain inconspicuous.

We arrived in Germany and stayed in an area referred to as
Lager. Hundreds of people waited in this area until they were
granted a place on a ship. Our fear was great. We were concerned that the communists would discover us there.
Periodically, particularly in the late evening hours, the communists would enter the area carrying their lists. They called out
names of individuals who were on a blacklist and hauled them
away. Everyone knew where they were taken—Siberia!

*"O LORD my God, in thee do I put my trust: save me from
all them that persecute me, and deliver me" (Psalm 7:1).*

One evening, the communists called out "David Dyck?"

My father was aware that they had his name but they did not
have his picture. After they called his name several times, my
father stood up and called out himself: "Where is David Dyck?"

He showed great courage and ingenuity. He asked the question again. The others in our group followed his lead. They too,

looked around for David Dyck. The officials were bluffed and concluded that the Dyck family had already left. Soon after the officials left the area, we boarded a ship for Canada.

Praise God! He had watched over my family again.

"I will not be afraid of ten thousands of people that have set themselves against me round about" (Psalm 3:6).

Later, when the Russians realized that they had been deceived, the border was closed and Lager was cleared. All the people who remained in Lager after we left were sent back to Russia. We were the last family to leave the country at that time.

... let all those that put their trust in thee rejoice: let them ever shout for joy, because thou defendest them: let them also that love thy name be joyful in thee. For thou, LORD, wilt bless the righteous; with favour wilt thou compass him as with a shield (Psalm 5: 11, 12).

Long after we were settled in Canada we learned of my uncle's death. He had died in Siberia at the hands of the communists. When we left our village, we had to leave everything standing as it was. My uncle, who lived on a farm in the area, lied to the officials on behalf of my father and his family. In order to "buy us time" for the escape, he told the officials that we were put in quarantine because of a contagious disease. When the officials learned of his deception, he was sent to Siberia.

Our freedom was bittersweet because our ancestors sacrificed themselves so that we could live—both my grandfather and my uncle gave their lives for the family.

"Greater love hath no man than this, that a man lay down his life for his friends" (John 15:13).

Two

My Family
in a Foreign Land

We started our new life in the spring of 1930. We arrived in Canada just as the depression was sweeping across the land. Our ship docked in St. John's, Newfoundland, and it was recorded in the statistics somewhere that we were a family of "five aliens with $25 to their name."

"...he will be our guide even unto death" (Psalm 48:14).

We boarded the train for Alberta and after a very lengthy ride, we arrived in Grassy Lake. My grandparents were there to meet us at the station. My mother's parents had come to Canada before my family. They became established in the foreign country and provided a home for us when we arrived.

In preparation for our arrival, my grandparents cleaned up an old chicken coop. It was about twelve by sixteen feet in size. Father soon built a kitchen onto the existing structure and, eventually, larger living quarters were added and a basement built underneath the kitchen.

From the kitchen, steps leading down to the basement were accessible by lifting up a wooden door. It was constructed by cutting out a part of the floor. A chain held the door up in place when entry to the basement was required. We stored food in the basement because it was much cooler down there and we did not have electricity.

When we arrived from Russia, there was David, Martha and myself. Later, Walter and Agnes were born. Rudy followed. With six children, we needed more bedrooms so we children helped Dad build two bedrooms onto the house. Dad built a framework that resembled the foundation used for pouring cement today but cement was not affordable. Instead, we filled the space with straw and over the straw we poured a mixture of mud, manure and water. Once the mixture was poured, it was the children's job to march over it in our bare feet until it was well trodden and secured in place.

In order to set properly, the mixture stood and dried for a good week. In weekly intervals, we added another layer of wall on top of the pre-existing one. Repeating this process, we created a wall six feet high. We were scared to march along the form, as the wall grew higher and higher but Dad encouraged our continued participation by reminding us to imagine our new bedrooms. Primitive homemaking, perhaps, but that wall was still standing fifty years later.

"For every house is builded by some man; but he that built all things is God" (Hebrews 3:4).

The part of the country where we lived was subject to strong windstorms. One time, we took refuge in the basement of our home. It was not safe to go upstairs because the wind was so fierce. We prayed and waited for the wind to die down. On one occasion, all of a sudden we heard a loud bang. When the storm passed and we were able to go upstairs and investigate, we found the outhouse had been lifted by the wind and smashed against the house, hitting the bedroom wall.

The basement was a roughed out area, a dugout by today's standards, but we were grateful for it the day it kept us safe and out of harms way.

"And there shall be a tabernacle for a shadow in the daytime from the heat, and for a place of refuge, and for a covert from storm and from rain" (Isaiah 4:6).

Since I was the oldest, I was the first to start school. Flickinger School was located half way between Grassy Lake and Skiff and named after the Flickinger family, who had donated the land to the community.

I started school at seven, the normal age back then. Dad walked me to school the first day, a mile from home. From then on, I walked alone each day. On a pleasant day, I loved to walk along and look at the plants and flowers. I also enjoyed looking at the sky and watching the clouds. The fence line served as my marker. It ran half of the way to the school. The rest of the route was not marked but it became familiar over time.

In the winter, I journeyed without the benefit of my guideposts. I monitored my steps by looking at the weeds poking through the snow. One day the ground was a blanket of white because it had been snowing all day and, without benefit of the weeds, I lost my direction on my way home.

There was a huge rock about half a mile from home. One end of it was pointed and it measured about the size of a dining room table. We used to refer to this rock as "Goliath's Grave". After walking about aimlessly, unsure which way to turn, I turned to God and began to pray, then looked around once more and spotted something that looked familiar. There before me was Goliath's Grave and I remembered which way it pointed so, with God's help, it directed me home. By the time I arrived it was late and night was falling. Everyone was relieved to see me but my father scolded me for choosing to go to school on such a stormy day.

In the end, God had made a path for me to follow and kept me safe and secure. He was my rock.

"The steps of a righteous man are ordered by the LORD*" (Psalm 37:23).*

21

School lunch was a limited menu. Each day I would take two slices of bread and butter. When the butter was not available, my mother would spread "geraivin" on my bread. It was made from ground up pig fat. My stomach could not tolerate such a fatty substance so I opted to eat plain bread instead. My mother felt so badly for me, but there was nothing else for her to offer.

Every year, our family looked forward to a special treat. Poor families that came from Russia were given two gunnysacks full of B.C. apples. We were so grateful and happy to receive all that fruit. They were odd-sized ones that could not be sold and most of them were tiny. But sometimes we would discover a big apple somewhere in the mix. Our eyes would grow large with delight when we spotted it.

I loved school and I wanted to learn. My family, like other Mennonite families, spoke High German at home. At school, we spoke English and were reprimanded for speaking German.

At the time I was introduced to reading, I was experiencing blurred vision. It was discovered that I needed prescription lenses and was told that I had to wear my glasses all the time. We were poor, so finding money to buy glasses was a challenge. The teacher informed the school board that I had to have the glasses in order to progress in my reading. My father was very concerned about someone else providing for his child. He felt he had to buy the glasses for me, but it was such a hardship for the family.

I was very happy when I was able to see words clearly. Finally, I was able to learn to read.

When I arrived home from school, I would eat a snack of bread and butter. If the cows were dry there was no butter so I would eat my bread plain. My younger brother would plead with me to tell him about what I had learned at school each day.

"What words did you learn today?" he would always ask.

As I would begin to share with him, my father would instruct me by saying, "Go and teach the cows. You need to do the milking. Your brother can listen while you do your work."

One snowy day, David, Martha and I walked to school together. Everything was fine on the way to school but walking home was a different story. We left the school and walked about half the way home before stopping at a neighbour's home to warm up for a while. David and Martha were often found together. This day was no different. They decided to start off for home without me.

Here I was, walking alone in another snowstorm. Along the way from the neighbour's farmhouse to our farm, I had to walk through a valley. When I came out of the valley on the opposite side, the wind was very strong. My feet were very tired and were aching from the cold. I experienced weakness in my feet, which was not common to other children of my age. It was directly related to the rickets condition that I had developed as a baby. I also felt pain in my chest that day. Later, this pain was determined to be a heart problem, but at the time, I was not aware of what was causing it.

I was straining to move myself against the wind. The fatigue and the pain became so great that I was uncertain whether I could continue. I decided to move myself off to the side of the road, reasoning that I could avoid being run over by a vehicle that might be passing by. I thought it was best to rest there for a short while.

A neighbour, who was not partial to milking the cows, decided to renege on his responsibilities. He chose to walk to our farm for a visit and discovered me fast asleep in the snow. He picked me up and I awoke with a start. He carried me to safety, saving my life. My family was surprised to hear where he had found me and were grateful to him. Once again, God saw me through another storm.

This neighbour was the recipient of much harsh judgment by others. His habits were outside the boundaries of the typical farmer. On a snowy day, God used that man to save my life. I feel indebted to a man who decided to depart from his ordinary routine. Where would I be today if he had not allowed himself to move out of his usual patterns?

Often, I have thought of how wonderful it is that God can use any one of us. I pray that He has blessed this man through the years. Only God knows.

Psalm 139 is very precious to me. God knows my every need. Even when I was asleep in the snow, I was not hidden from His view.

As a child, I always loved the summer season and would often watch other children running and playing. I always thought it would be so much fun to skip rope but every time I attempted it I got hurt. My ankles were not strong. Because of the rickets, the bones were not well developed and my ankles wobbled and I flipped over when I tried to land on my feet. Naturally, landing on one's feet is an integral part of skipping rope. It was disheartening to learn that this activity, which looked so easy and fun when I observed others doing it, was not possible for me. It was so disappointing. At that stage of my life, I learned that my bones were not made for a whole range of physical activities that other children took for granted.

I was starting to question why I was so different from other children and asked my father many times why I could not be like the others. He told me all about the rickets and the limitations it placed on my activities. During school recess time, I used to hide in the bathroom so that I would not be asked to play. I knew that I could not participate in the games. I felt so cut off and alone.

"I will praise thee: for I am fearfully and wonderfully made: marvelous are thy works; and that my soul knoweth right well" (Psalms 139:14).

Three

Becoming a Winner of Souls

Our family attended a Mennonite Brethren Church. The church families rented school space where we had church services each Sunday morning. My first Sunday school teacher, Mary Penner, was very loving. I loved her and she loved me.

Henry Thiessen was my Sunday school teacher when I was a teenager. One of my earliest memories of our church was Mary Penner's wedding to Henry Thiessen. I thought their wedding was the most beautiful thing I had ever seen.

Today, Henry and Mary Thiessen have a son named Willard. Willard and his family live in Winnipeg, Manitoba. They have a television program, aptly named *It's a New Day*, which is familiar to many believers.

Going to church was actually quite an ordeal for us. Our family did not have a vehicle so we had to walk a mile to the school and from there, we road with another family to church in the box of their truck.

After the dawn of the New Year, 1936, Mom and Dad went to a church meeting. They walked to the school where a neighbour picked them up and then they drove to the meeting together. I remained at home and cared for my younger siblings. The church meetings continued over three or four consecutive evenings, led by visiting ministers who came to share the gospel. After our church Bible study concluded, these same ministers would move to another church like our own. In this way, Bible study continued from church to church throughout southern Alberta.

When Mom and Dad returned home from their first church meeting they were very encouraged. It was common practice in our home to have evening devotionals and that evening we proceeded as usual. Mom and Dad were excited to tell us that God was doing new work in our church. Several Christians had confessed their sins.

Following devotionals that night, David and Martha stayed behind with Mom and Dad. They accepted Jesus and asked Him to forgive their sins and come and live in their hearts.

I went to bed ahead of the others. When I was not able to go to sleep, I sensed that the spirit was working in me. I believed in my heart that I was a Christian. The spirit reminded me about that "big apple", which came flooding back to my thoughts. When we received our bags of apples, I had taken the biggest one and had not told anyone about it. The spirit reminded me that I had stolen the fruit. Then I knew that I was a sinner.

Following this moving of the spirit, I had a vision of Jesus on the cross. He looked so loving and yet at the same time, so sad. Feeling convicted, I took my place on my knees by the bed and prayed, asking God to forgive me. I asked Jesus to come and live in my heart too. I was eleven years old.

A short time later, the bedroom door opened and my father entered. He came to my bedside and started to ask me about accepting Jesus, as David and Martha had just done.

"I just finished asking Jesus," I said.

"When?" he asked.

"Just before you came to see me," I replied.

He looked at me with questioning eyes, but I knew the truth. My father turned and left the room. I think he was sad because I had not prayed with him.

The next morning when I awoke, I felt wonderful, so new and alive! I asked God to give me a verse and I received the following scripture:

"But as many as received him, to them gave he power to become the sons of God, even to them that believe on his name:" *(John 1:12).*

What a confirmation! I knew that I had received Him and that there was something new in my life. I was happy. Praise God!

Most of the time, our home life was very difficult. Many demands were placed on me because I was the oldest child. My mother needed my help and although I wanted to help her, the time it took to complete the tasks assigned to me left little time for my studies. My reading ability progressed very slowly. Reading was difficult and I knew I did not read my Bible as much as I should.

In addition to my home and school responsibilities, I experienced physical problems that were very taxing. We continued to have food shortages. Our garden was just starting to be productive. Pain and nutritional deficiencies made life a burden. When my mother would question me about my physical ailments, I started to lie in order to avoid enduring some "so called" remedy. At fourteen years of age, I reasoned that the medicine was worse than the condition.

But lying to my mother was not sitting well with my conscience. One night, I had a dream and in this dream the Lord came to take his saints home to heaven. I was shocked to learn that I was left behind. I arose from my bed and ran to see if my mother was still there. She was there, sleeping in her bed. Relieved that it was, in fact, a dream and not reality, I confessed my lies to my mother the next morning. Afterwards, the burden of lying lifted and I felt cleansed once more.

The following night, I had another dream. In this dream, the Lord came to take his bride home. I went up in the air and stood before the Lord. I understood that even though I had been a believer for a little over two years, I was empty-handed before my Lord. I had done nothing for God. At that moment, I was reminded of a German song, *Only Leaves, Only Leaves, And No Fruit – For The Lord.*

That second dream was a life-transforming experience. I immediately committed my heart to serving my Lord. I vowed to read the word faithfully and to win souls for Jesus. I constructed a calendar, which would provide a place to track my Bible reading and the lessons I learned from scripture. I made notations on the calendar on a daily basis. I developed a disciplined approach to learning about God through the word.

I was very frightened to learn that I had stood before God and I had done nothing for Him. From then on, I was a soul winner. Like Joseph, who, as a child, had dreams and did not understand them until much later, I knew that my dreams were very important.

My life was changed.

A few months after my fourteenth birthday, I was water baptized in Old Man River. Afterward on the sunny Sunday afternoon we had a picnic on the island.

A short time later, I became concerned for the children at the school who did not attend Sunday school. I invited all of these children to our home. They came Friday afternoons, after school. I led a Sunday school in our house for the next year and a half. Some of the children from our church attended and my siblings joined in as well. We sang children's Christian songs and I told Bible stories. I helped the children understand how to accept Jesus into their hearts. Some of the children accepted Jesus during that time, including my youngest brother.

We had a large herd of cattle on our farm. One cow had very big horns and a very temperamental disposition. One of my siblings got too close to her once and was hurt badly. The cow knocked my sister to the ground and proceeded to roll her away with its horns.

One day, my father asked me to go and get the cows from the field. I told him that I was scared. He told me to fetch a big stick and go and get the cows. I followed his instruction but I did not realize that my stick had a crack in it. The cows were quite a distance from the yard. I was able to herd them in the right direction but one cow went astray and I had to use my stick to redirect it. Then another cow went off course and I had to do the same thing. This happened over and over on the way back to the farm.

At one point, I saw that my stick had been worn down and was no longer useful. That was when the cow with the big horns approached me, coming closer and closer. In defence, I raised my arms over my head and cried out "Jesus, help me!" I looked at the cow and demanded, "Stop in the name of Jesus!"

That cow came within two feet of where I was standing and stopped in its tracks! It looked at me, turned around, and walked away, ignoring me and following the other cows back to the yard.

Just as God controlled the animals that went into Noah's ark two by two, in the same fashion, He controlled this one cow. This experience really spurred on my faith. I knew God could do the impossible.

Holy cow, God is good! Let the name of the Lord be praised!

During the early spring, a young man, a couple of years older than me, asked me to go on a date with him. This young man was familiar to me because he attended our church. I was stirred by the invitation because it was the first time I had ever been asked out on a date. I knew that I needed to make a decision. I had learned that this young man was involved in behaviour that was not moral in the eyes of God. My grounding in the word, and my evolving relationship with the Lord through prayer, gave me the strength to do what was right and to remain true to the commitment I had made to the Lord.

Reflecting back on that time, I think of all of the teenagers today who are faced with difficult choices during their adolescent years. I am grateful to God for leading me on the right path and keeping me righteous.

I am reminded of John 15, which tells us that He is the vine; we are the branches. We can only have strength as we thirst for the word of God.

Wherewithal shall a young man cleanse his way? by taking heed thereto according to thy word. With my whole heart have I sought thee: O let me not wander from thy commandments. Thy word have I hid in mine heart, that I might not sin against thee (Psalm 119: 9, 10, 11).

One day, I went to my father and told him that the neighbours needed to know about Jesus.

"They don't want to know," he said. "They don't care."

"Someone needs to tell the English speaking neighbours," I said. "You are a minister. You can tell them about the gospel."

At about the same time, the Lord ignited a gift of poetry in me. My first poem read as follows:

Why do you stand idle here?
Many others, the gospel yet must hear.
Go and tell them.

One Sunday afternoon, God put it in my heart to visit the neighbours in their homes. In response, I put on a big jacket. It was tight at the waist but loose at the top. I was able to conceal my Bible and my songbook in the loose part of my coat. I told my family that I was going for a ride on my bicycle but I did not tell them of my plans.

I mounted my bicycle and rode away feeling trepidation because I was unsure of myself and I was so very shy. I called on God to help me and the Lord said:

"Teaching them to observe all things whatsoever I have commanded you: and, lo, I am with you always, even unto the end of the world." (Matthew 28:20).

When I knocked on the first door, I was welcomed into the home. I came into the kitchen, unzipped my coat and removed my Bible and songbook. I asked if I could share something with them.

"We would like to hear what you have to say," one of them responded.

I started by singing a song or two. After that, I described my testimony and how I became "born again". I then gave a short teaching from the Bible and we talked about how to find salvation in the Lord. My neighbours told me they had never heard the message before. They wanted to take time to think about it.

The next Sunday, I went for another ride, stepping out for God. I rode uphill to the first farmhouse but was disappointed when I learned that no one was at home. I left a note and a tract in the door to alert the residents of my visit and rode to the next farm. This time, someone was at home and I was invited into the house.

Sunday after Sunday, I travelled on my bicycle, from home to home in the area telling stories of Jesus and His great love. One Sunday afternoon, I arrived at my neighbour's doorstep but before I could knock, the door opened and I was asked to come into the house. I was led into the big living room and asked to wait there. I was given something cold to drink while I waited. I did not know why I was waiting, but I took the time to talk to God. I asked Him to help me respond to the situation before me. It was a sunny, warm, harvest afternoon.

31

The next thing I knew, combines had been shut down, farmers had washed up, and they were approaching the room where I was sitting. As they filed into the room and sat down, I called out to God. "Oh God, I want to fall through the floor. Look at all of these people."

God coached me by urging, "What if this is the only time they get to hear the message?"

I mustered up my courage and began with a couple of songs. I told my testimony just as I had done at the previous visitations. After that, I presented a Bible lesson. When I finished, a couple of individuals approached me. They told me that they wanted to know more.

"We cannot go to your church because we do not speak German," they said. I told them there was a good church in Skiff.

"They will welcome you there," I said.

About two weeks had passed when I received a phone call from Mrs. Thiessen. She informed me that a couple of my neighbours had visited their church in Skiff and they had told her I had directed them there.

The first couple, who visited the church in Skiff, was now "born again". Mrs. Thiessen went on to report that another family had visited, and now the whole family was "born again".

> *Now the God of peace, that brought again from the dead our Lord Jesus, that great shepherd of the sheep, through the blood of the everlasting covenant, make you perfect in every good work to do his will, working in you that which is well pleasing in his sight, through Jesus Christ; to whom be glory for ever and ever. Amen (Hebrews 13:20, 21).*

In time, most of our neighbours came to the Lord. I was so happy. I was so grateful that God helped me to overcome my shyness on that sunny Sunday afternoon.

Later, it came to my mind that God had placed the burden on me to tell others. God did not put the burden on my father's heart because his language was such a barrier. I was riding my bicycle around the countryside breaking ground for Jesus. I think it was a bicycle built for two.

But ye shall receive power, after that the Holy Ghost is come upon you: and ye shall be witnesses unto me both in Jerusalem, and in all Judea, and in Samaria, and unto the uttermost part of the earth (Acts 1:8).

When I finished Grade 9 at Flickinger School there was no high school nearby for me to attend and I wanted to go to Bible School. At seventeen years of age, I attended the Mennonite Brethren Bible School in Coldale, Alberta. I enjoyed studying the word of God very much. During my third year, we also studied psychology, learning about guilt and what it can do to the human spirit.

It was then that I understood why my father was the way he was. He was prone to being reactive and lash out at me physically. I determined that he was unable to shift his thinking from the days in Russia. In those days, he was not able to share the gospel because of the communist regime. When he lived in Canada, it was difficult for him to move his thinking into our new reality. The guilt consumed him.

When he saw my outward expressions of love for the Lord he was not able to encourage my efforts. He lamented, "If only I had of this... And, if only I had of that..." And so it was.

I came to understand that my father loved me, and the abuse was a product of those very harsh days in Russia, and I forgave him any wrongdoing.

"Forgive, and ye shall be forgiven" (Luke 6:37).

When I learned scripture that I thought conveyed forgiveness, I shared the scripture with my father. My heart hoped that he would come to forgive himself and be set free from the bondage of the past. I prayed for him often.

Later, it was clear to me that my father did get liberty. His behaviour communicated that he was more relaxed and that he was at peace. Again, God answered my prayers, helping my father to forgive himself and to find peace in his heart.

"If the Son therefore shall make you free, ye shall be free indeed" (John 8:36).

Four

My Mission Grows

During the winter, I learned that distant relatives of mine had gone to Africa to do mission work. I also learned that this couple had come home but was not planning to return. I prayed and asked God, "Why are these people not returning to Africa? There is such a need there."

"You prepare," God replied.

"Ask of me, and I shall give thee the heathen for thine inheritance, and the uttermost parts of the earth for thy possession" (Psalm 2:8).

Later, I learned that the couple had not returned to Africa because the woman had developed cancer of the skin.

During summer intervals, I taught children at Vacation Bible School. I worked with a mission in southern Alberta, west of Medicine Hat and close to the mountains. Along with an experienced teacher, I lived in the teacher's residence. We taught lessons in the classrooms located at the front of the school.

Our days were divided into three specific activities. In the mornings, we taught lessons. In the afternoons, we visited homes in the area, where we shared the gospel. In the evenings, we planned activities for the following day.

As we shared information over the two-week period, the children displayed greater interest. By the time we were ready to leave, several children had accepted Jesus. Before we left, I instructed those children who had accepted Jesus to spend time together. I urged them to get together regularly, to read the word, to develop their understanding, and to encourage each other.

When we returned to the area two years later, the children reported with enthusiasm that they had followed my instructions. As well, the children informed us that a pastor had visited the area twice a year to deliver sermons to the residents.

The response to our home visits was variable. Some people welcomed us and were attentive to our message about Jesus. In other homes, our words fell on deaf ears. One young girl, a teenager, left a very strong impression on my heart. She cried and cried and stated openly, "I want Jesus so much but my boyfriend will get mad." I was disturbed about her situation and I hated to leave her.

"He, that being often reproved hardeneth his neck, shall suddenly be destroyed, and that without remedy. In the transgression of an evil man there is a snare: but the righteous doth sing and rejoice" (Proverbs 29:1,6).

Two years later, I was saddened to find this same young woman married that same man. It was evident from her flat expression that she was not happy. Life had drained from her face. Over the years, I have thought about that woman and the many times she prayed to God to place grace on her life.

The life of that young woman offers a lesson for all of us. When God is speaking to your heart, do not turn Him away. He is calling you for a reason. He has a greater plan for your life than you can know at the time.

"Almost thou persuadest me to be a Christian" (Acts 26:28).

These are the words that King Agrippa spoke to Paul. To be almost saved is not sufficient. In the hymn, *Almost Persuaded*, written by Philip P. Bliss, we hear this message loud and clear.

Almost persuaded, now to believe;
Almost persuaded, Christ to receive;
Seems now some soul to say,
Go Spirit, go Thy way,
Some more convenient day
On Thee I'll call.
Almost persuaded, come, come today;
Almost persuaded, turn not away;
Jesus invites you here,
Angels are lingering near.
Prayers rise from hearts so dear;
Oh, wanderer, come!
Almost persuaded, harvest is past!
Almost persuaded, doom comes at last!
Almost, cannot avail;
Almost, is but to fail!
Sad, sad, that bitter wail –
Almost, but lost!

After three years, I graduated from Bible School. At my graduation, I spoke with an individual from the Mennonite Brethren mission and inquired about going on a mission to Africa. He asked about my health, noting that I had problems walking.

"Don't bother to apply," he told me flatly.

I felt very discouraged by his dismissal.

I had a friend who attended Prairie Bible Institute (PBI), a mission school in Three Hills, Alberta, and started to regain my hope.

During the summer months, a dreadful flu-like condition spread throughout Alberta. In some people, like my brother, it caused pneumonia. In others, like me, it affected the eyes. They were weakened by the sickness. As a result, I could not read at all for a whole month and had to have the prescription for my glasses changed.

The following winter, I began my studies at Prairie. While enrolled at PBI I became involved in a special prayer group for Africa. Missionaries from PBI, who went out to work in Africa, sent their prayer requests to our group. We prayed for their needs.

My previous Bible studies focused on memorization of scripture verses in preparation for doing personal work with people. At Prairie, we studied the gospel stories that depicted how people came directly to Jesus for help. Jesus was able to address their problems at the source. I thought the approach Jesus used was a very practical way to help people. He knew their heart so He was able to meet inner needs.

About a month into my time at PBI, my eyes became weaker and weaker.

When I contacted my father to inform him that I needed money for a new pair of glasses, he informed me that, "We don't have the money."

He was shocked because he had just paid for a new pair of glasses before I started school at PBI Other students at PBI learned that I needed glasses but that I did not have the money to buy them. They encouraged me and said, "Well, you need to pray that God will provide for your needs."

I remained true to their direction and prayed to God. I went to have my eyes tested and a prescription for new glasses was ordered. I waited in faith and continued to attend my classes as usual. One or two days before my glasses were expected to be ready, I returned to my dorm room and found an envelope on my desk. Inside, I found the money I needed to pay for my glasses.

"And all these blessings shall come on thee, and overtake

thee, if thou shalt hearken unto the voice of the LORD *thy God"* *(Deuteronomy 28:2).*

I do not know where that money came from. What I do know is that God saw to it that I could see clearly as I read His word.

It was a wonderful school year at PBI I learned a great deal both about the Bible and about missions in Africa. As the year was coming to a close, I received a phone call from my father to notify me that my mother was burned in an accident. I wanted to go to her but he told me I had to remain at PBI for the mission conference, which concluded each school year.

At the conference, I saw my former Bible school teacher, who was surprised to see me there. He told me that my mother was still in the hospital. At that point, I felt very ill at ease. It was difficult to keep my thoughts focused on the conference presentations.

I approached a representative from the African Inland Mission to learn about going to serve in Africa. He asked me questions about my health and, again, like the other man, told me, "Don't bother to apply!"

I was depressed by his response. Coupled with my mother's condition, my distance from her, and now his reaction to me, I felt disheartened.

The conference ended and I was on my way home. We stopped at the hospital in Coldale to see my mother. Although I was grateful to be near her, the smell of rotting flesh was over-powering. I learned that a gas iron had exploded and my mother's face was burned. At the time, my father was nearby and dressing to go outside. He had a leather jacket in his hand. When the explosion occurred, he rushed to my mother's side, wrapped her face with the jacket and extinguished the flames. I was told that my brother fainted when he entered the room and smelled the stench.

I was heartsick for my poor mother. All that we could do was pray for her recovery, and thank God that the tragic incident did not take her life. Praise God!

When I arrived back at the farm, I assumed all the domestic responsibilities for the seven family members. My world had been all about studying so the kitchen and cooking all seemed foreign to me.

One month later, when mother arrived home from the hospital, she needed time to recover. I was thankful that she was home. She gave me directions and helped me to know what to do, instructing me about meal preparations and other work. I was so grateful for her presence and her input.

The following autumn, my family was not able to send both of us so my brother David went away to Bible school. I remained home with my mother and turned to God, and searched my heart to determine the next steps on my path. Now that I could not go to Africa, what was I to do?

In my communications with others from Prairie Bible Institute, I learned about an orphanage in Wetaskawin and decided that if I was not able to go to Africa, perhaps I was able to help in an orphanage right there in Alberta. I applied to Bethany Homes for Children.

I started my position after the Christmas holidays, assigned to perform the cooking duties. I loved it at Bethany. There was such a wonderful spirit in the home. About seventy people worked together, cooperating with each other and living as a family. The children were from broken homes where their parents were either separated or divorced.

When I started at Bethany, the money for supplies was inadequate. After the Christmas shopping season, many families did not make donations. The first three months in my role as cook, I learned how to make dishes with the limited resources available to me. Meal preparations required creative instructions from God. I prayed and God directed the meal plans and the children provided feedback about my cooking. They said they were satisfied. The adults and I prayed and fasted.

One week after fasting, the administrator phoned me to say, "There is money in the mail today. What do you need?"

"Everything!" I replied. "Finally, I can cook decent meals!"

I loved my time at Bethany so much! As it turned out, my spirit was strong but my bones were not. During my stay, I made repeated visits to the chiropractor, an associate of Bethany Homes for Children, so I did not have to pay for my treatments. My rickets condition continued to follow me like a bad plague. After my last visit to the chiropractor, my administrator was informed that I had to quit my position immediately or I would be crippled for life.

At twenty-three years of age, after only six months at Bethany, something else was taken from me. I returned to the farm but part of my heart remained at Bethany. I was so heartbroken when I had to leave. I yearned to be there. Once more, I looked to God for comfort, strength and direction. The Lord showed me that He never closes one door without opening another.

At the heart of my being, I identified my desire to help others. I found a correspondence course that was being offered from the Chicago School of Nursing and set my sights on working in a hospital. I completed the course, then found a position in Taber, Alberta. Following that, I worked in Lethbridge. In both positions, I worked as a nurse's assistant. In Lethbridge, I had the added responsibility of managing a ward for children. Even though I worked under the supervision of a nurse, the majority of my tasks were completed independently.

But the work was hard labour and, again, I was not able to continue for very long due to my health. The administrators were not pleased when I submitted my resignation. They were satisfied with my performance but the cost to my health was too great. Sadly, I had to walk away. I sighed a heavy sigh and asked God, "What now?"

Looking back on that time, I know that if I had not had

strong faith, I would have broken down right then and there. Enough was enough!

Thankfully, God and I had a strong relationship. He always encouraged me. My relationship with the Lord allowed me to move along, even if it was just one day at a time. The King of Kings was my strength. He encouraged me and kept me.

Over the years, I have always enjoyed the pursuit of learning. This time in my life was no different. The next leg of my journey pointed me in the direction of teaching. I reasoned that a teacher was not required to lift children like a nurse does. I opted to finish my high school credits and head off to teacher's college.

I completed my Grade 10 close to home and Grade 11 in Coldale. My education continued in Winnipeg, Manitoba. It was in Winnipeg where I discovered that I could complete my Grade 12 and then earn my teaching certificate during the summer months. With my temporary teaching certificate, I was qualified to teach for one year.

Considering all of the setbacks I had experienced, I must admit that I entered the teaching vocation with a certain degree of skepticism, but, knowing that the Lord was with me, I jumped in with both feet. I had an opportunity to teach on a trial basis before investing much more of my time and energy. I believed I would be in a better position to judge my suitability for the profession after my school year ended.

My first teaching assignment was located in a northern community called Thicket Portage, Manitoba. This remote village was approximately half way between The Pas and Churchill. The school was small, housing only two classrooms. Grade 1 was the largest group because the children from the area had sporadic attendance. If the parents went hunting or fishing, the children accompanied them. I was assigned to teach Grades 2 through 8. This represented about thirty children. The teacherage was used as a classroom because the Grade 1 class was so large.

Alternate housing arrangements needed to be made. I was blessed to learn that the North Canada Evangelical Mission was located in Thicket Portage. It had a large house where I was able to find accommodations within walking distance to the school. One of the missionaries at the mission was the Grade 1 teacher. We developed a good relationship and worked well together.

The village of Thicket Portage was set in a wooded area. It had one store, one school, and the mission. The mission was small and the people were transient. Those who were involved in the mission did not feel gifted for praise and worship. We found a way to share our gifts. They taught me the Cree language and I led the worship. We had one Sunday service. I had an accordion in those days and would sing and play. During the week, we held one activity night for the children.

Of special remembrance to me was the Christmas season. It was too far for me to return home to Alberta for Christmas. I prepared the children ahead of time and then invited them to join the mission workers for caroling. The houses in Thicket Portage were organized in the shape of the letter "U". We started caroling at one end of the village and, as we moved along, people started coming out from their homes. They listened and some of them reported that they stayed out the whole evening. The captive audience compared the sound to "a group of angels singing in the night."

The gift of caroling worked wonders to heighten my reputation and to build my acceptance within the community.

One day, a resident from the village, someone unknown to me at the time, approached and asked, "Have you ever had a dogsled ride?"

I answered, "No. Is it safe?"

The stranger assured me that I would be safe and helped me position myself on the sled. It was great fun as he drove me around the community, the snow crunching under the weight of the sled.

Time flew by and Easter came in a hurry. During the weekend, I took the train to Churchill and discovered two missions there. I was intrigued as I looked out over the Hudson's Bay. Many ships were lined up in the bay and the whales moved about in the icy waters. I enjoyed my weekend visit very much.

After finishing my school year, and before leaving the area, I ran a small Bible camp at a nearby lake. I had brought a limited supply of groceries for the camp, which became more evident as the number of people arriving grew larger and larger. But God knew my situation and provided for my needs. Before long, a man arrived with a large fish and everyone went away satisfied.

After leaving Thicket Portage, I stopped in The Pas to have all of my teeth extracted. I had developed gum disease, also known as pyorrhea. I remained in The Pas just long enough to get my dentures, and then left to teach Vacation Bible School in Flin Flon. The rest of the summer was spent in Coldale, Alberta, where my parents had made their new home.

In September, I returned to Winnipeg and completed one year of teacher's training, living in the dormitory at normal school. I secured a part-time job at the school doing various kitchen duties at mealtimes. In turn, I was able to reduce the costs of my training. The closest Mennonite Brethren Church was too far away to allow me to return to the school in time for the lunch meal. As an alternative, I started attending the Alliance Church on Portage Avenue.

The church initiated a poster drawing contest aimed at attracting children from the community to Sunday school. My poster received first prize. In recognition of my drawing, I was awarded a book entitled *In His Steps*. I have treasured that devotional book throughout the years.

I participated in the Christian Association at the university, then known as United College. Once a week during the school year, another teacher and I taught children from the neighbourhood about Jesus. This activity was refreshing because it offered a change of pace and a new environment. I enjoyed witnessing to the children and helping them to learn about Jesus.

At the close of the school year, I was given a teaching assignment in Churchill. My position was scheduled to begin the following September. Knowing my compass was set for the fall schedule I left university and flew to Lethbridge on my first-ever plane ride. I was scared, to say the least. Throughout the journey, I sang quietly, "He has the whole plane in His hands. He has the whole plane in His hands. He has the whole plane in HIS HANDS....!"

The Lord looked after my bird in the sky and the plane landed safely. My brother was surprised to see me because he did not know that I was going to fly back for his wedding. It was wonderful to celebrate the occasion with family and friends and to be away from school for a spell.

I spent the summer at my parents' home and dedicated my time to preparing materials and resources for the coming school year. My preparations included many prayers to God because I anticipated that my new position would be very demanding. I knew I needed God's grace.

"I will instruct thee and teach thee in the way which thou shalt go; I will guide thee with mine eye" (Psalm 32:8).

Five

My Challenging Family

The summer passed quickly and by mid August I was travelling on the train to Churchill. It was an extremely long journey. On the way, I conversed with some native people who were also heading to Churchill and bought a beaded belt from one of them. It was handmade of course. I thought it would be a visible demonstration of my desire to learn about the culture and traditions of the people.

A school board member met me at the train station. As it turned out, this woman was the wife of the United Church minister in Churchill. She showed me where to find lodging and I got settled in my new home.

On Sunday, I went to the Mission Church. Later in the day, I was invited to join the pastor and his wife for dinner. I arrived at their home to discover that they had invited Jacob Peters. Jacob worked at the army barracks. After dinner, we visited for some time. Jacob offered to walk me home since it was getting dark outside and he was heading in the same direction on his way back to the barracks. When we arrived at my doorstep, I thanked Jacob and wished him well on his bus ride to the army base. I went inside and immediately made the necessary preparations for Monday.

At twenty-nine years of age, I was teaching Grade 7 and 8, and administering the school as principal. The first two months of my assignment were enjoyable. The students were cooperative and pleasant enough.

Then, I invited the pastor from the church I attended to lead the Remembrance Day service on November 11. I was not aware that in previous years the minister from the United Church had led the service. I believe that it was this change of leadership that set a whole lot of things in motion.

Following that service, something changed in the school environment. For one thing, the students' behaviour became disruptive. It was unclear to me why their behaviour would change so drastically. Teaching required discipline as well as instruction. My feet responded poorly to standing for long periods of time. In order to cope, I needed to sit down at various intervals during the school day but maintaining discipline from behind a desk was not successful. The students were aware of my dilemma and they took advantage at every turn.

Sunday by Sunday, I attended my church. Jacob Peters showed an interest in me and over time, our relationship grew. Throughout the fall months, he and I spent time visiting with the pastor and his wife.

As Christmas approached, Jacob and I decided to travel to Coldale. Naturally, before we left Churchill we stopped in to visit the pastor and his family. The children had the chicken pox. Without further consideration, we left for Coldale to spend Christmas with my family.

I went to the Lord and asked, "God. Should I marry Jacob?"

The Lord replied, "I will be with you in it."

Deciding that I had the blessing of the Lord, I informed Jacob that Africa comes with me. Jacob and I were married December 28, 1954, with one little glitch. We had to inform the guests not to bring their children to the wedding. My husband had developed the chicken pox. Three days after the wedding, we boarded the train and travelled to Morden, Manitoba. There, Jacob's family and friends referred to him as Jake.

Jake's father had not been a good provider. As a result, Jake's mother had had to move about the community begging for food and various items needed for the home. At some point, she succumbed to the stressors in her life and was admitted to the mental hospital in Brandon, Manitoba. All of her children, including Jake, were placed in foster homes.

When we arrived in Morden, we had an after-wedding service with Jake's family and friends. It was at this service that I met someone who had played a very special role in Jake's life. I was introduced to Jake's spiritual mother. He thought so highly of her. When a family tragedy had occurred just two years earlier, she had been there to comfort Jake. Shortly thereafter, she led him to the Lord.

Following the celebrations, Jake and I returned to Churchill and moved into our new home, which we had purchased before leaving for Coldale. It was located next door to the North Canada Evangelical Mission.

Jake returned to his duties as cleaning service man at the army barracks and I resumed my duties at the school. By mid February, I experienced a tubal pregnancy. I was taken to the army hospital to have surgery. The school board personnel learned of my medical emergency when an announcement was broadcast over the radio. The broadcaster made an urgent plea for blood donations. That transmission over the airwaves marked the end of my teaching career. My position was assigned to another teacher.

I needed time to heal from the insult to my body. Later, at a follow-up medical visit, my physician diagnosed me with a thyroid condition. He was alert to my symptoms: extreme fatigue and inability to perform daily tasks.

Time passed as I healed from my surgery and regained my strength. Both Jake and I wanted to have a family but we were unable to conceive. At that time, we became aware of a baby in the community, malnourished and neglected, who needed a warm and nurturing home. We accepted him into our home when he was five months old and, just before Christmas, we adopted him as our son and named him Allen Loren Peters.

We returned to Coldale for the holiday and introduced our new son to everyone in the family. By this time, he was responding to our attentiveness and loving care and Jacob and I were enjoying family life. Just when we were thinking about another adoption, I discovered that I was expecting a baby. Allen was three years old when our baby boy was born. We named him David.

The nursery at the hospital where David was born had been subject to an unknown infection, which resulted in many deaths, so it was closed and disinfected, reopening some time later. Our baby was spared but many babies were not. I was thankful to God for my healthy boy. God answered my prayers yet again.

In my spare time, a woman from church walked with me to a neighbouring community on the other side of the tracks. We had conversations with the native people who lived there. We inquired about their lives and asked if they needed any kind of help. We encouraged them and shared the word of God. We wanted them to know that God cared and we cared about them.

On Sunday afternoons after church, we enjoyed our lunch meal along the shore. Our sons enjoyed running along the waterside and amongst the rocks. I used to marvel at how they never slipped and broke a leg on the watery surfaces. Despite their freedom to run and play, we were very attentive to the boys when they were near the bay. A neighbour's son nearly met his death when the tide changed and left him perched on top of a rock. The warning was there for all of us to heed.

I was pregnant a second time when Jake was transferred to Winnipeg. It was 1962 and we had lived in Churchill for eight years. The army packed our belongings and paid all the expenses to move us to the city. Army personnel did all of the work involved in the move. The help was such a blessing to me. Since I was expecting, it would have been a real burden for me without their assistance.

Our new residence was on Parkview Street, in the St. James area of Winnipeg. Jake started working immediately to cover holiday periods for other workers. The move was a blessing all around. Living in the city meant being closer to relatives and friends. We liked our new home and it was close to a neighbourhood school for Allen. Lydia, our daughter, was born on February 1, 1963.

One night in March, I awoke in the middle of the night. I had developed a habit as a child of covering my head when I was sleeping. When I took the covers from my head, I detected a heavy odor in the house. I tried to arouse my husband but he did not respond when I shook him. The cover had protected me from whatever was in the air.

I quickly opened the door and hurried about the house waking everyone from sleep and the effects of the fumes and managed to get everyone outside. It turned out that our furnace had malfunctioned. We were able to take refuge at a neighbour's home until it was replaced the following day.

God woke me up in time. Praise God! He watched over my family once again.

When Lydia was approaching her second birthday, we discovered that she had enlarged tonsils. The discovery was made when she was sitting on her aunt Lydia's lap. At one point, Lydia laughed and because she was facing her aunt, her mouth was open to full view.

"I've never seen such large tonsils!" her aunt exclaimed.

I responded that I had thought her fussing was due to teething problems.

I waited a few days, thinking that the problem would resolve itself but Lydia developed a very high fever. The next day, her fever was even higher. She cried and cried and could not be comforted. When she opened her mouth, I saw that pus was forming.

Our family physician was travelling from one office to another, so he offered to stop in and see Lydia en route. I was grateful that he was able to accommodate us at home. The doctor expressed his concern and ordered antibiotics immediately. As well, he scheduled a date for Lydia to have her tonsils removed. He instructed me to monitor the lines of infection in her mouth. If they were still present the day before the surgery, I was to have the surgery postponed.

The day before we were scheduled to go to the hospital with Lydia, I noticed that the lines of infection remained in her mouth. I felt certain that God would allow the surgery to be performed as scheduled. The next day, I arrived at the hospital and left Lydia to have the operation. While she was there, I went to a Pentecostal church and asked for healing prayers for my daughter. As I returned home, the phone rang. It was Lydia's doctor. He informed me that the surgery had been completed.

"Lydia had the biggest tonsils I have ever seen in a little girl," he said.

Sadly, the pus moved from the tonsils into Lydia's kidneys and bladder. The condition was not operable. The poor child endured trial after trial of antibiotics. Finally, after three years, the doctor reported that the last course of antibiotics would be administered.

"If this antibiotic is not effective," he said, "then we have run the gamut of available medications to treat the problem."

"I guess it is time for more prayer," I told him.

The final antibiotic remedied the situation. Both Lydia and I were grateful.

My husband believed that since he provided the money for food and shelter, I should provide the funds to cover any other expenses. The medical costs were great. The financial need was a burden for three years. I completed various sewing tasks as a way to pay the medical expenses.

One day, Jake complained of a headache. I made an appointment for him to see the doctor and he went that same day. The doctor admitted him to the psychiatric ward at the Health Sciences Centre. His physician informed me that Jake would have to stay in the hospital for an extended period of time.

"I don't know when, or if he will ever come home," he said.

I was devastated. I cried out to God and God told me to sing. I learned to sing through my tears. I was obedient to God and in turn, God honoured my faith. A month later, Jake was released from the hospital. He was at home and the doctor was perplexed by his recovery. I knew it was God's intervention that brought my husband home. Jake was back at work a month after leaving the hospital.

"But he was wounded for our transgressions; he was bruised for our iniquities: the chastisement of our peace was upon him; and with his stripes we are healed" (Isaiah 53:5).

In the early spring, Lydia developed an infection again, and our family physician told me that Jake really needed a holiday because of his nerves. He said that Lydia would be cared for in the hospital while we were away. Lydia went to the hospital and Jake and I took the boys on a holiday to Niagara Falls. We were gone for four weeks. While we were away, my friend visited Lydia in the hospital every day. She took one home cooked meal to the hospital each day because Lydia was not interested in eating. In this way, my friend, who was suffering from cancer herself, monitored Lydia's appetite, nutritional needs, and provided some TLC.

I have remained grateful to that friend, Mrs. Johnson, to the present day. While we were on our holiday, I could be at ease knowing that someone was checking in on my dear daughter. When our holiday was over and we returned to Winnipeg, we learned that Lydia was healthy again and could come home from the hospital.

When Jake had been in the hospital, the doctors were able to determine that he had schizophrenia. Our home life was very volatile at times because his disposition was explosive and vulnerable to the influence of the disease. His behaviour was unpredictable. We never knew what part of his personality was going to surface or when he would lash out at us.

I was able to manage our finances and sort out our debts while Jake spent time in the hospital. Still, he took a second job driving taxi. He seemed to need the additional activity and was not opposed to the extra money it earned.

On Saturdays, while Jake was driving taxi, I would initiate activities and outings for the children and myself. This was my window of opportunity to bring joy and relaxation into our lives. Saturday and Sunday afternoons we were often found frolicking and enjoying a picnic lunch in the nearby park. We liked to ride our bicycles, and sometimes we rode to the zoo. The children enjoyed those trips; each child had a favourite animal to observe.

One Sunday, the children and I arrived home to find that Jake had locked us out of the house. I phoned a social worker to secure some form of assistance. The social worker had been assigned to our family when Jake came home from the hospital. In response to the situation, a family conference was held. Two social workers and two pastors attended the meeting. The professionals offered to support me in filing separation papers. I felt that God wanted me to stay in the marriage. I remembered God telling me that He would be with me in it. The professionals warned Jake that he would be removed from the home if any similar incident should happen in the future.

Since I did not have a driver's licence, the children and I started to attend the Bethel Baptist Church, which was located just across the back lane from our home. It was there that I met Mr. and Mrs. Graves. They were very kind to me and the children and we developed a friendship through our association at the church.

I was not able to drive a car due to problems with my neck. When I tried to turn my head, my vision would become blurred. One time, Jake tried to teach me how to drive because he did not believe I couldn't do it. He changed his mind when I asked him which yellow line I should stay beside.

One day, while listening to the radio, I heard an advertisement about the Canadian Sunday School Mission Camp. The speaker indicated that the camp was open for children of eight years and older. I thought it would be a wonderful experience for our son, Allen. I called the phone number that was provided to learn more about the camp and was told the camp was held at Gimli, Manitoba.

As an incentive, children could have their camp fees paid if they memorized scripture. Allen was so excited about the prospect of going to camp that he memorized over 200 Bible verses. Memorization seemed to come easily to him. As the time approached for him to go, he became a little uneasy about the idea. I phoned the camp office to find out if we could tour the camp ahead of time so that Allen could familiarize himself with where he would be going. I was pleased to learn that a family camp was being held the week before the children's camp and that we were welcome to participate, and that is what we did.

We travelled to Gimli and toured the campsite. I was given the job of cleaning an old stove that had been donated to the camp. The stovepipes and vents were clogged. I spent a whole day cleaning that stove and in the end, when it was started, it worked very well. In fact, it worked well for many years to come.

God of the Impossible

Family Camp concluded and it was time for everyone to pack up and leave. We looked around and could not find Allen anywhere so we assembled a search party. Finally, Allen was found. He was so thrilled with the camp and the great outdoors that he did not want to leave. The camp counsellors explained to him that everyone had to leave so that the grounds and bunkhouses could be cleaned before the children came for camp. He was welcome to come back the following day, after the cleaning had been finished.

We dropped Allen off at the children's camp the next afternoon. He was so happy to be spending time there. We left him knowing that he was comfortable and in good hands.

Over the years, all of our children attended that camp during the summer months. They enjoyed the activities and the natural environment. Jake and I became very involved in the family camp, which was a blessing to our family.

Allen and David also attended Boy Scouts and learned many things of interest to young boys. They were instructed on how to tie knots, how to light a fire without the benefit of matches, and how to make a tent out of tree branches. One day, they asked if they could make a tepee style tent down by the river's edge. I agreed to their plan. They rode their bicycles along Portage Avenue to where the city centre ended, then travelled on a road that ended at the Assiniboine River. They constructed their tent out of tree branches just as they had learned in Scouts.

It was a beautiful evening so the boys decided they should move their sleeping bags out of the tent and sleep under the stars. They reasoned that they should then burn their tent to provide the warmth of a fire. While the tent was burning, the sky became cloudy and it started to rain. After the rain, just before sunset, I decided to enjoy a bike ride and headed down Portage Avenue. As I approached the end, I looked to my left and I saw two young people approaching.

"That cannot be my boys," I thought.

I continued on my ride and when I returned home, I found my two sons in the house, soaking wet.

Jake had a habit of screaming at our children when they were outside. He called them names and, in turn, our children started using the same names on other children who lived nearby. The neighbours started to complain about Jake's erratic behaviour so Jake decided that he wanted to move out of the area.

In 1969, we moved to a house on Brock Street in River Heights. It was close to the base for Jake. The school was nearby and there was a park across the street from the house. We were blessed to be in such an advantageous location.

In order to make the down payment on our new home, Jake returned to Churchill to sell the home we owned there. He spent his holiday time repairing it and sold it immediately after the repairs were completed.

While Jake was in Churchill, a neighbour took the children and me to a place called Oasis. Oasis was aptly named. It was a time away for all of us, from the city, from the tension in our home, and sadly, it was time away from Jake. We absorbed every moment of this natural environment. We spent two weeks immersed in nature, picking berries, splashing in the water, and enjoying the warmth and comfort of the sunshine.

Although the children really enjoyed their new home and their outings to the park across the street, their father continued to create stress within the home. One day, God gave me a brilliant idea. In one corner of the basement, I hung a pillow from a cord. On one side of the pillow I drew a picture of a pig. On the other side, I drew a picture of a cat. When it was evident that the children needed to release some tension, I invited them to go downstairs and box the pig or pet the cat.

This pillow proved to be an important form of release for the children. Sometimes they boxed the cat and patted the pig but I was not about to argue. I think it gave them some satisfaction to go against my instruction and be rebellious. If it was a way to help them cope, it really did not matter which animal they hit. Either way, the pillow was a hit with my children. I knew they needed some form of control in their lives. Their rebellious behaviour was being channelled in a constructive way and that was all that mattered.

In 1970, Jake decided the family would move into an apartment near Cathedral Street and Main. He assumed a position cleaning the apartment building and, of course, he volunteered his sons to help with the jobs. Jake believed that this move would provide more money for the family because the apartment came with the cleaning position and the house on Brock Street could be rented out to tenants. These tenants brought in more than money—cockroaches soon infested the house.

One year later, when the tenants complained of the cock-roaches, Jake evicted them. Our family moved back into the house on Brock Street but, of course, it had to be fumigated first. The children were pleased to be back in their familiar neighbour-hood and returned to their old schools.

In 1974, Jake had to retire from his janitorial position with the army. Immediately, upon his reaching the maximum twenty years of service, the army terminated his position. Bethesda Church needed a janitor so Jake took the assignment and Bethesda became our place of worship. The children partici-pated in the boys and girls club at the church.

Allen, our oldest son, was leading a disturbed existence. He was coming and going and we never knew where he was or what he was doing. Sometimes, this variability went on for days at a time. One Saturday afternoon, I felt a real burden to pray for him. I prayed that God would spare his life and his mind. I prayed that Allen's brain would be preserved. By three o'clock that same afternoon, the burden lifted.

Several days later, Allen arrived at our home. His girlfriend was at his side. After some casual sharing, I asked the girlfriend, "What happened this past Saturday afternoon?"

"Oh Saturday!" she responded. "It was horrible. I was not certain if Allen was going to live or die. He took such a large overdose. It was really strange though. Right about three, he was doing much better all of a sudden."

What a confirmation! I told them about my prayers for Allen and the heavy burden God placed on my heart that Saturday afternoon. I told them how I felt the burden lift right around three.

While we were living on Brock Street, we had four teenagers in our home. We had three children of our own and one foster child named Ken. This was a major responsibility and my health was not supporting me. I had a growth at the top of my spine near the base of my skull. It affected my right arm, rendering it next thing to useless for any purposeful activity. It was very difficult to do my housework.

At a visit to the doctor on a Friday, he told me I had rheumatoid arthritis. The X-rays showed the growth. After diagnosing the problem, he sent me on my way.

"You have to learn to live with it," he said.

My nerves were challenged that day. It was the same day I learned that my parents were coming to visit. They had indicated their visit would be within the coming weeks but had not provided an exact date. How was I supposed to prepare? I needed help.

On the Monday morning, I was reading the psalms. One verse said, "God helps the needy." At that point, I looked skyward and exclaimed, "God. I am really needy."

God reminded me that Jake goes to work and the children go to school. God instructed me to pray and fast for three days. For three days, I prayed and I fasted. I cooked meals for the family but I did not eat. God directed me to read Matthew 5, 6, and 7. The Lord really ministered to me through the scriptures. I understood that I was very needy. My need stemmed from the abuse that I had endured at the hands of my husband. As I continued to read the word, I became aware that I had not forgiven him. My lack of forgiveness startled me.

As I read the word during those three days, it seemed as if God did an operation on my spirit. On the fourth day, I got up as usual. Jake went to work. The children went to school. I looked to the Lord and asked, "What do I do now? The three days have passed." And the Lord said, "Your house is a mess. Clean it up."

Being obedient, I started to clean and tidy. After a while, I walked into the kitchen and saw that it was 11:30. Soon, the children would be home for lunch. I told myself that I needed to hurry and get things prepared.

All of a sudden, I was taken aback. I had been working all morning. My arm! My arm! My arm was working again! I stopped in my tracks and reached around to touch the back of my skull. I moved my hands up and down and groped the back of my neck. The lump was gone! It was amazing! I was so grateful. I had been obedient and God was faithful.

At the time of my last visit to the doctor, my physician had referred me to a bone specialist. He had forwarded my X-rays so that the specialist could review them prior to my appointment. I went to the specialist on the appointment day and when my name was called, I entered the doctor's office.

"What can I do for you today?" he inquired.

"Well. I used to have a problem with..." I responded, describing my symptoms.

As I continued describing my condition, the doctor interrupted me to ask, "What do you mean, you used to have?"

"Doctor," I responded, "I believe God has healed me."

The doctor pretty much ignored my comment and said, "Since you are here, we are going to do a series of X-rays."

I consented and the X-rays were taken. The doctor asked

me to wait and left to review the images. Shortly after, he returned wearing a big smile. When he compared the first set of X-rays with the second set, it was clear that the growth was gone. God had healed me. What a wonderful testimony for God!

When Mom and Dad came for their visit my mother exclaimed, "My, your house is clean, and with four teenagers to manage!"

When I was healed, I thanked God and got to work. In the end, I was pleased with the state of my home when my parents arrived.

There seemed to be a history of heart problems on my father's side of the family. His younger brothers experienced heart attacks. After father's heart attack, he was uncertain of his time left on earth. He began to talk about his life and share information about our family history. We learned about how my grandfather was murdered when he took my father's place on the wagon in Russia. The wagon was not found but my grandfather's dead body was located somewhere in the countryside.

My father was a stern man who was rigid in his thinking. It was difficult for him to forget the suffering that he and his family members experienced in Russia. His heart felt the pangs and was affected by the great range of the human experience.

"He shall not be afraid of evil tidings: his heart is fixed, trusting in the LORD. His heart is established, he shall not be afraid, until he see his desire upon his enemies" (Psalm 112:7, 8).

I was at church one Sunday morning when I heard the Lord tell me, "You have had your father for five more years."

I felt an urgency to give thanks and express my gratitude to the Lord for his blessing. It had been five years since my father had his heart attack. He had recovered to such an extent that he was driving his car again. The family was truly grateful for the improvements in his health.

As I entered the kitchen after arriving home from church, the phone rang. The voice on the other end informed me that my father had just passed away. Once again, I thanked God for the additional time with my father, and for the forewarning that I received that day at church.

We attended Bethesda Church, which was close to our home on Brock Street. Jake was the janitor at the church. Naturally, while cleaning the church, voices were overheard and things were said. Some words that were spoken did not still well with Jake. From what he described, it was apparent that there was much disunity in the church. This was very upsetting to both Jake and me.

I prayed for the church. It was clear to me that this was not the appropriate climate for a church. Gossip was raging with the intensity of a strong wind. While I prayed for peace and unity to restore the foundations of the church, God shared a poem with me and instructed me to post the poem in the church, at a time when I would not be seen by members of the congregation. No person was to know who put the poem there. The paraphrased poem *A message from God*:

> *God is our gardener, wise and tender.*
> *He makes each flower, after its kind.*
> *It matters not what kind or colour.*
> *He made me, but my roots, what are they like,*
> *under the ground.*
> *May I not be odious, but sweet fragrance send.*
> *Heed His Words! Love one another, my friends.*

In James 1:26, we read:
"If any man among you seem to be religious, and bridleth not his tongue, but deceiveth his own heart, this man's religion is vain."

The church, which was ready to break apart, found a time of restoration after the poem was posted for the membership to read.

While we attended Bethesda Church, our foster son, Ken, was "born again". He was born with a crippling condition and required a wheelchair for mobility. His mother was not able to take care of him and he joined our family when he was thirteen. Our daughter, Lydia, was a nurse at heart from the time she was a little girl. She was generous with her nurturing qualities when it came to helping Ken. They related well with each other.

Jake's custodial job at Bethesda was a term position. One year later, he was assigned to the Mennonite Brethren Church (MBC). A house next door to the church was provided with the custodial position so we sold our home on Brock Street and moved into our new accommodations. Lydia was excited about the move to the new church. She was an avid reader and was ready for a new library of books to study.

The church house was close enough to Portage Avenue that we had frequent callers from the neighbourhood. People knocked on our door and asked for money. One day, two aboriginal young men appeared on our doorstep. I asked them to clean up the hedge clippings and broken branches in the front yard. These fellows worked very hard for over an hour. They completed the task thoroughly. I invited them into the house for something to eat and afterwards paid them for a job well done. They went on their way and I was pleased with their efforts and the results.

Other times, people came to our door and asked for bus money. When I asked them to help with some tasks before getting the money, they told me, rather sharply, to do my own work! These individuals were a striking contrast to the young men who had cleaned the yard and worked so hard when asked to lend a hand.

Ken was baptized at the Mennonite Brethren Church. A woman at the church took a special interest in him. She was a professional teacher and spent time with Ken evaluating his learning potential. She reported that he had a fine mind for learning and she believed he had just not been challenged in his former educational placements.

In order to provide a better educational opportunity for Ken, Jake left his position at the church and we moved out of the area to the Northgate Trailer Park. Ken was blessed by the move and by his new school, and graduated Grade 12. Shortly after his graduation, he moved to another home.

While we lived at the trailer park, David attended high school at Mennonite Brethren Collegiate Institute. Following his graduation, he went to Bible School in Saskatchewan. David enjoyed Bible School but he missed Anita, who was his sweet-heart from Winnipeg. After Bible School, David and Anita were married.

Lydia finished high school. Naturally, she pursued a career in nursing, completing her training in Winnipeg.

Six

Beyond Family, Beyond Borders

As for me, I became involved in a Christian Writer's Club. A local television station approached our club and asked that someone from our group offer a Christian television program. I resisted the idea because I was convinced that no one would want to watch me on television. I believed that I was ugly. God began to work on me about the program. He even gave me a name for the show. He wanted the program to be called "Sunshine at Home". I thought this was absolutely ridiculous because there was little sunshine in our home. My husband's behaviour and mental problems left little room for sunshine.

God understood my needs and directed me to focus on "Good Food for the Body, Soul, and Spirit".

I struggled with the idea of a television program for at least three months. Finally, I said, "Yes. I will do the program." Amazingly, I then found peace. I was not able to find peace until I obeyed God.

I told God, "If my husband says yes to the program, then I will do it."

I was quite certain that my husband would not agree because he was disagreeable about most things, particularly those things that were not his idea. We taped the first program. My husband and I viewed the program with the television representatives.

Afterwards, he turned to me and said, "I think it is very good." I knew then that God would be victorious. The one time that I wanted my husband to disagree with me, he agreed instead.

A distant relative of mine offered to play the piano at the taping of the first television program. She played and I sang. When the taping of the music was finished, I told her she was free to leave if she wished but she wanted to stay for the taping of the program also. I finished the taping and together we left the studio.

On our way that day, she communicated that she had been helped by the program. She related that God had really spoken to her while she listened. My attitude about doing the program shifted because I realized that it could be a blessing to others. Three months later, we were informed that the television station representatives liked the program content. They appreciated the focus on healthy recipes and nutrition. They thought the information was very practical. Other program presenters provided information about vitamins and minerals. At that time, nutritional supplements were not as "mainstream" as they are today.

By the conclusion of the fifth year, I asked God if I could quit the television broadcast and he said,

"...*open thy mouth wide and I will fill it*" *(Psalm: 81:10).*

After ten years, I asked God if I could stop the program. I knew where the scriptures were located, so I conveniently avoided certain sections. On that very day, someone came up to me and said, "Open your mouth wide and I will fill it." God repeated the same scripture that He had given to me when I tried to quit five years earlier. Every week, God gave me a topic, a lesson, and a song for the lesson. During that time, He refined my ability to hear His voice and learn His teachings. He gave me songs to communicate the information.

At one point, I thought another woman I knew could do a better job than I could so I invited her to be on the program. After the program concluded, I was told, "I'm sure glad you're doing the program and not that woman who joined you today."

So, with that, I told God, "I will wait for you to tell me to stop the program."

There was no stopping God. He always had the last word.

Years later, the woman who answered the phones for the program told me we had wonderful comments and responses from the viewing audience. She said that we had many answers to prayer through "Sunshine at Home". I was not aware of the extensive way that God had used the program to reach others who were in need of His word.

In 1989, at sixty-five years of age, Jake retired. We moved our trailer to the Christian Enrichment Family Camp area, near Pilot Mound, Manitoba. Shortly before we moved, the television station reduced my tapings to once a month. This was a blessing because we were able to attend to many needs on our monthly trips to the city. We drove into Winnipeg, taped the television program, did our grocery shopping, and visited with family and friends. God looked after the practical side of things.

While we lived in Pilot Mound I enjoyed watching the Christian programs on television. One morning, I was watching "It's a New Day" when God spoke to me.

"You have not checked yourself the way a woman should," He said.

I kept postponing the direction and continued watching my programs. God was persistent and continued to repeat his warning. Finally, I followed his directive and found a very tiny lump in my breast. Three days later, we made our monthly trip to Winnipeg. After taping the television program, I went to see my doctor. My husband thought I was addressing my heart problem.

The following week, I found myself on the operating table. While I was waiting for the doctors to prepare for surgery, I began singing to the Lord. I knew that the Lord would minister through the hands of the surgeons. I was not afraid. I left my condition with the Lord and put my trust in Him.

I overheard the physicians commenting, "Listen to her. She is going to have cancer surgery and she is singing."

My behaviour prompted the doctors to ask me how I could be singing when I was waiting to have cancer surgery. I took the opportunity to witness to the physicians and nurses. They questioned me about how I was able to detect such a small lump and I informed them that God had told me. I told them about salvation. They had removed a lump and I had planted a seed.

Within two weeks of having my operation, a man who had agreed to take the television program telephoned to inform me that he could not do the taping. I found it difficult to do the program but God helped me through it. Since I had been in the hospital, I had not been able to prepare any material. Instead, I gave my testimony over the air waves that day. My broadcast was a shout of praise for the Lord and the work He had done in my life.

Back in Pilot Mound, I needed time for healing. After some time had passed, I asked God why I was taking so long to heal.

"You are not as sick as the church is," He told me. "You are on your back. Take this time to pray for the church."

So in obedience to God, I spent my time praying. The burden on my heart was very heavy. God was doing a physical healing in me and a spiritual healing in the church.

My husband and I became very involved in the Christian Enrichment Family Camp. Personnel changes were made when sin in the camp was exposed. Some members thought the personnel changes were all that was standing in the way of the camp's progress. They believed that once that obstacle was removed, the camp was set to soar but God told me to say, "We can only go as high, as we go low."

In other words, we must lose our arrogance and humble ourselves before the Lord. Throughout my involvement with the camp, God gave me words to share with the church members. At the church service, I communicated what God gave me. Some members were displeased and some were angry. Nonetheless, I gave what God gave me. Some members were very thankful for the guidance given by the Lord. I knew God was speaking through me. The words came from God because I kept my relationship with Him alive.

More recently, and some decades later, I encountered a fellow member from the family camp who told me, "You were such a blessing to the camp at a time when the members needed direction. God gave you the words to say and they were so right on."

"...he will be our guide even unto death" (Psalm 48:14)

One winter, Jake and I were asked to go to an orphanage in Mexico. We were substituting for another couple who had incurred injuries. In their place, we delivered many donations from Canada to the orphanage. One of my activities while in Mexico was sewing assorted linens and supplies. My husband helped in the print shop.

One afternoon, I went on a shopping trip to purchase souvenirs but the woman, who drove me to the marketplace abandoned me there. I thought we were going to the market together, but she informed me that we would meet after her dentist appointment.

Previously, I had been warned not to move about in that area alone, so I was fearful. I prayed and trusted that God would look after me while I shopped. I collected my souvenirs and met the woman at her car. We travelled back to the base where we were staying. Upon our arrival, the woman next door came running out of her unit. She exclaimed in a hysterical voice, "What have you been doing all afternoon? I have been in constant prayer. I have felt such a burden to cover you in prayer."

I looked at the woman and thanked her for her prayers and her obedience, and told her how I had spent my afternoon. I knew God had worked through this woman and once again, God had watched over my life. God had kept me out of the way of any harm.

> *For in the time of trouble he shall hide me in his pavilion: in the secret of his tabernacle shall he hide me; he shall set me up upon a rock. And now shall mine head be lifted up above mine enemies round about me: therefore will I offer in his tabernacle sacrifices of joy; I will sing, yea, I will sing praises unto the* LORD *(Psalm 27:5, 6).*

Back in Canada, we prepared for another move. This time, my husband had learned of a home for sale in Mather, Manitoba. It had a very large yard and was reasonably priced and he wanted to buy it.

"Well," I suggested, "God led us to the Christian Enrichment Family Camp. God should be the one to tell us to leave."

"Well," he replied, "you ask God then."

I prayed and read the word and God gave me the following scripture:

"*Ride on victoriously, oh mighty one, for the cause of truth....*" *(Psalm 45:4).*

I knew God planned for us to move to this new home. When our son Allen found out about it, he purchased our former home. Since the mobile home was close to the camp, we saw it as a blessing that Allen would spend time there. We believed that being near the camp would be a positive influence on him. We moved to Mather in the summertime.

Our new home had three bedrooms and was situated on one and a half acres of land. There was an old barn and one part of the acreage had a little park-like setting. It was a picturesque place. However, it did not take us long to learn that the fellowship in the area church was unfulfilling.

After getting settled in our new home, we travelled to British Columbia and took discipleship training from Youth With A Mission (YWAM) in North Vancouver. It was 1992 when we were invited to serve at a mission in Tahsis, on Vancouver Island.

One evening, we were invited out to dinner at the home of a fellow participant at the YWAM training. His wife told us to make ourselves at home. We were shown the library and I started looking at the book titles. I discovered a book about Skiff and took it from the shelf and leafed through the pages. I spotted the name Flickinger School.

I went to the kitchen and asked, "Who here knows about Skiff?"

The woman of the house answered.

"My maiden name was Flickinger," she said.

I was in the home of one of the neighbours I had witnessed to so many years ago! This woman was one of the neighbours who came to know the Lord through my community outreach. That evening, we experienced a very meaningful conversation during a time of fellowship.

Our God weaves the threads of time in such an intricate way. We never know when his cross-stitching is going to develop into a familiar pattern. His design is beyond our imagination and our description.

Discipleship training was informative and reflective. Many lessons were learned. One particular revelation has remained alive in my mind throughout the years. The Lord showed me that I cannot be controlled by someone else and also be controlled by the Holy Spirit. Serving two masters is not possible.

"No man can serve two masters: for either he will hate the one, and love the other; or else he will hold to the one, and despise the other. Ye cannot serve God and mammon" (Matthew 6:24).

Each year, at the close of discipleship training, YWAM had a special Angel Week, during which we exchanged names. The name you got was the name of your "angel". We were told to be attentive to words that encourage when we sought the Lord in prayer and instructed to find ways to share this encouragement with our angel.

Another woman and I noticed the actions of one particular woman in the group. She was always interfering with her husband's affairs and ordering him about. God gave me an idea. I shared the idea with the other woman and together we prayed about the couple and about their interactions. We decided to send this man a letter from an angel. God directed us to communicate the following message to this man:

"God has put you in the position of principal. God will equip you to do His will."

In a couple of days, there was a discernible difference in the behaviour of the principal. He was a changed man. As a teacher and leader he needed to change. He had been controlled by his wife instead of being led by the Holy Spirit.

YWAM involved three months of training. One of the three months was spent doing outreach in Alberta, both in Calgary and in Edmonton. While in Edmonton, we travelled to the poor area of the city and spent time talking with people on the street. On the drive to the area, I noted a woman sitting on a porch. Behind the porch was an apartment building. The place was neglected. As we drove by, the Lord told me, "That is where you are going to go."

We stopped and I got out of the car and walked to the porch. I sat down beside the woman and started to talk, telling her about Jesus.

"I need this," she said. "I need Jesus."

Just then, a fellow from the back of the building appeared in front of me. "No one preaches here!" he threatened, waving a switchblade back and forth in front of my face.

I turned my head away and prayed quietly. "God, send him away. This woman wants to hear about you."

Without hesitation, the man turned and ran away quickly. I was not afraid because I was concentrating on the woman. She, however, was frightened. After the man left, she was so afraid that she was speechless. All that mattered was that God had kept us safe from harm and that the woman had heard the gospel.

A group of people, including the couple who had driven me to the area, were watching from across the street. The couple told me later that they never took their eyes off of me, they were so concerned for my well being.

On another day, we distributed donuts to the poor and I found myself surrounded by four drunken men. They were badly scarred and their appearance was wicked. I discovered that I only had three donuts but there were four men. I gave one donut to the first two men. The next donut, I broke in half and gave the other two men a half each. That experience marked the first time that I ever looked into the eyes of someone controlled by the devil. It gave me the shivers. I have never been able to get that look out of my mind. For days later, I cried and cried and prayed for those men who were so lost in their lives. Their eyes made it clear to me, just what sin does to a person.

For sin, taking occasion by the commandment, deceived me, and by it slew me.
Now then, it is no more I that do it, but sin that dwelleth in me.

73

But I see another law in my members, warring against the law of my mind, and bringing me into captivity to the law of sin which is in my members (Romans 7:11, 17, 23).

During the summer months we returned to Mather. A short while later, we packed up and went to Bible Camp about 150 miles north of Prince Albert, Saskatchewan. The population was mostly aboriginal. At the camp, I taught crafts and led the praise and worship. My husband helped in numerous ways according to the need.

When one young aboriginal boy heard the gospel, he said, "I have been in touch with my native powers. I want to be "born again" but I do not want to lose my Indian power."

I was deeply saddened to hear this boy speak in this way. It represented a form of deception that exists in the world.

Ye are of your father the devil, and the lusts of your father ye will do. He was a murderer from the beginning, and abode not in the truth, because there is no truth in him. When he speaketh a lie, he speaketh of his own: for he is a liar, and the father of it. And because I tell you the truth, ye believe me not (John 8:44, 45).

After Bible Camp, we headed for Prince Albert on our way back home. Along our route, we noted that something was wrong with our vehicle. We were over 100 miles from Prince Albert.

"There is definitely something wrong with the car," Jake said.

"You drive and I will pray," I replied.

God watched us drive into the first gas station that we found in Prince Albert. As we drove up, the car broke down and came to a halt.

No matter where we find ourselves, whether it is in the south, in Mexico, the Pacific shores of British Columbia, or the wooded lands of northern Saskatchewan, God goes with us. Thank you, God. We appreciate your presence as we travel.

God loves to hear our praise. He loves a grateful heart.

Not long afterwards, we made an application to go to the School of Evangelism in Tyler, Texas, the following winter. We saw the leaves change four times that autumn. First, they turned north of Prince Albert, then while driving through southern Manitoba, again when we arrived in Tyler, and when we travelled to New Orleans for a short outreach. I loved that journey that circled through the turning of the leaves. Nature repeated itself over and over and over. What a joy it was to see a colourful canvas transforming across time!

Tyler, Texas held some interesting sights. We were in awe of the long bridges. We also noted that the graves were made of cement and all of them were erected above ground. We spent Christmas in Tyler, which was so far south that people said they had never seen snow. When I prayed, I told God that I would like a little showing of snow for Christmas. Much to my delight, God sent snow for His favourite little girl.

"Delight thyself also in the LORD; and he shall give thee the desires of thine heart" (Psalm 37:4).

Following the Christmas season, we made preparations for a trip to Nicaragua. The primary language there is Spanish and I had learned some while we were in Mexico, but in Nicaragua, we had to learn much more in order to visit homes and determine if the residents needed a Bible. While we stayed in Nicaragua, the song, "Do you know that Jesus loves you?" was translated into Spanish.

When we went to the hospital to sing, I was appalled at the conditions there—rats!!! As we were singing, we went from room to room. At one point, we noticed that our audience kept getting larger because the people from the previous rooms were following us to the next. "The more the merrier," was the message of the day.

We returned to the base where we were staying and I was having a rest when I felt a shaking beneath me. I was puzzled by what I could feel, which was a minor earthquake.

On another day, we visited an orphanage where my husband engaged in a game of ball with the boys and the director led me on a tour. At the end of the tour, he turned to me and said, "I hear that you have been at other orphanages. Can you give me some pointers as to how we can make improvements in ways that will not require much money?"

I looked at the man and God spoke through me, giving me many ideas. He showed me a number of practical changes that could be made. I advised the director based on what God told me to share. God reminded me of one idea and then another and another. I knew the help was from God and not from me.

Upon our arrival back at the base, we decided to visit the little park across the street to determine if we could use their sound system and perform a short drama. We were told that we could and returned to the base and made our arrangements for the evening.

Later, when we entered the building at the park, we were surprised to find people there. We were not aware that anyone else would be present. About 1,000 people were standing about.

We continued as planned with the younger ones in our group performing the drama. I moved through the crowd and handed out tracts. The second drama started, but before it was finished, there was a disruption near the back of the room. Our leader and another man were having a not-so-pleasant conversation.

"I don't know how this happened!" the other man said.

He was so angry he kept repeating the same message over and over again. As he spoke, his voice got louder and louder. Tension in his voice developed and his body language was not friendly. God kept that leader confused and his mind was confounded. He was not able to think clearly. He was paralyzed by his intense anger; he was simply beside himself.

About twenty members were in our group. We packed the drama supplies, the tracts and our belongings and hurriedly left the building. We ran and jumped into the van. After excusing himself, our leader rushed out to the van and we sped out of the parking lot and returned to the base.

Back at the base, our leader informed us that we had crashed a communist recruitment party. The building was full of guns! We escaped and not one shot was fired.

God protected us. We shared the gospel and distributed tracts. As we drove away, I noticed that not one tract was on the ground. The seeds were left for God to nurture. We were grateful for our safety. The following day, we left Nicaragua.

"But the LORD your God ye shall fear; and he shall deliver you out of the hand of all your enemies" (2 Kings 17:39).

Jake and I returned to Mather once more. This time, we sold our property and purchased an eighteen-foot trailer and moved it to a spot beside Faith Temple in Winnipeg. I guess all of the excitement caught up with me. Shortly after getting the trailer in place, I experienced heart problems and was taken to the hospital. The physicians injected dye into my arteries and discovered that they were blocked. The doctors tried several times to clear them but were not successful. They informed me that it was a miracle that I did not have a heart attack because the blockage was so severe. I encouraged the doctors to try one more time and I prayed. I told them that I was needed at Faith Temple to teach others how to lead the children's Vacation Bible School the following week.

One month later, my chest hurt and the arteries were blocked again. I was taking eight heart pills a day. Before I could seek medical attention, I got a phone call from YWAM in North Vancouver. They informed me that a group of seventy or eighty people were arriving and asked me to come and cook for them. They said Jake could assist me in the kitchen. I thought, well, I don't have time to be stopping in to see a doctor right now.

My children warned me not to travel and told me I was not well enough to take on such a great responsibility.

"God will equip me if He sends me there," I said.

Jake and I headed out on yet another journey. We went south of Winnipeg and travelled through the United States to British Columbia. After a time, our van needed attention. A mechanic informed us that it was going to take quite some time to fix the problem.

Jake and I found a church and through that church, we were led to a very needy person, a woman who had a real heart for people in the jails, particularly for those on death row. She wrote letters to the inmates about God's love but church members were opposed to her ministry.

The woman asked me, "What shall I do?"

"God always reaches out to sinners," I encouraged her.

This woman and I spent time together. I taught her and tried to help her understand what God would want. I showed her that she would have to form a right attitude towards the church.

One day, the woman said to me, "You can go. I am ready. I am ready to let you go. I can stand with God's help."

On the same day that the woman felt grounded in her faith, the mechanic contacted my husband to say that the van was ready. It had not been ready to roll until the woman was ready to stand. It was so interesting to observe God's timing in the events of our lives.

We arrived at YWAM and performed our service in the kitchen. Jake and I had to buy the groceries and supplies as well as do the cooking. My vision was blurry because I had had a cataract operation on one eye but not on the other. When Jake and I were shopping, I had to remember what colour of shirt he was wearing so that I could spot him in the store.

Helpers were assigned to our kitchen but they were more of a hindrance than a help to us. Once a month, there was a managerial meeting but we were often forced to leave the meeting because our helpers in the kitchen were not responsible workers. That experience was challenging and some people were critical of the menu. They wanted food that tasted good but they seemed to be unaware of healthy meal plans. I thought they would be wise to pay attention to the healthy aspect of the meals we prepared for them.

I have learned that healthy food choices lead to healthy hearts. To this day, I have never had that heart operation. Furthermore, I used to take eight heart pills a day and now I take none. Thank you, God, for healing my heart.

Once the dishes were washed and the utensils were put away, we left the experience behind us.

Our next home was located on Vancouver Island in a place named Tahsis. One morning, Jake went outside to meet the day. In what seemed like a turnaround, he ran back inside and threw himself on the couch. The ambulance was called and delivered Jake to the hospital nearby. Within three hours, my husband was gone. He had succumbed to a heart attack.

Upon reflection, I remembered a scripture that God had given to me prior to our move to Tahsis.

"...Except a corn of wheat fall into the ground and die, it abideth alone" (John 12:24).

After Jake's passing, I understood why God shared this verse with me.

Prior to Jake's death, we had applied to YWAM and were scheduled to serve in Maui, Hawaii. The circumstances had changed. Jake was gone, but I decided to continue with our plans for mission work. A woman friend of mine accompanied me on the journey.

We arrived in Maui and made our contact with the representatives from YWAM. I was assigned to work in the kitchen but I did not feel that God wanted me there. One day while I attempted to close a window, I fell backwards and broke my left wrist. As a result of that fall, I was not able to work in the kitchen so I was asked to serve in the school.

I remember one young boy from the school. His story has

stayed with me throughout the years. This young boy was known to be quite a behavioural problem. One day, his mother was asked to come to the school so that the teacher could speak with her about her son. After the teacher spoke with the mother, I asked the mother if she would like to go for a walk to the church. We walked side by side and talked along the way. God put it in my heart to share a different perspective about the boy with his mother.

I began by telling her some of my observations. I told her about a number of her son's abilities that I thought were positive and worth cultivating. The mother looked at me with surprise on her face. This mother had never heard anything about her son that was positive. We prayed together in the sanctuary and then left to make our way back to the school. It was like shining a new light on the situation for this woman. She and I walked back to school but now she had a renewed sense about her.

Improvements did come for that boy and I know this because the mother made the effort to keep in touch with me long after I had left the island. We became long-distance friends.

Another story of interest centred on homeless people. People from the street ate at the YWAM dining room. Individuals approached me to talk while they were having a meal. Later, after the homeless left the dining room, other mission workers approached me and shared, "You are like a magnet to the people from the street."

Being that the people were living on the street, their personal hygiene left a lot to be desired. Their clothes were dirty and their hair was tangled and matted from neglect. While I was in their presence, God was working on me. One day, He gave me an idea. He directed me to make Valentine's Day cards for the people from the street. Inside, I wrote to them about God's love. When Valentine's Day came along, I handed out the cards to each of them as they entered the dining room. They were overwhelmed. Many of them came up to me and told me that they had never heard anyone say that they loved them. Some of the people reached out to hug me. My initial reaction was to withdraw but God nudged me to return their hug and so that is what I did.

God's love reigns supreme no matter where we go and no matter who we meet. We are called to demonstrate love to others. After all, isn't that what Valentine's Day is all about? After all, isn't that what life is all about?

While in Tahsis, my anti-inflammatory medication, which I was taking to alleviate pain in my knees, caused problems with my stomach. When I got up one morning, I noted abnormal bleeding. Friends drove me to the local hospital. From there, I was flown to the hospital in Nanaimo. Tests revealed three major bleeding ulcers in my stomach. The attending physicians blamed the anti-inflammatory medication.

From that point on, I was not able to eat spicy foods or use anti-inflammatory medications. Instead, I began taking a supplement of calcium magnesium with vitamin D.

Seven

Off to Africa

The following autumn, I flew to Winnipeg to see Mr. and Mrs. Graves off to Africa. When they saw me, they told me I looked healthier than they had ever known me to be. They invited me to join them in Africa the next spring. Mr. Graves outlined the preparations I would need to make. I returned to Tahsis and initiated the necessary arrangements.

I was going to Africa. My long awaited dream was coming to pass.

Shortly after my mother's one hundredth birthday, in March 1996, family, relatives and friends gathered in a big hall in Coldale, Alberta. Together, we celebrated this noteworthy milestone. The celebration was catered and a feast of food was enjoyed. Mother's mind was clear and the party was wonderful for her. Naturally, she experienced fatigue by the end of the day due to all of the excitement. It was a special occasion for all of us. The reunion gave many opportunities to share and reminisce about distant memories.

At the conclusion of the celebration, I shared with my family that I was planning to go to Africa. Due to the many health problems that I had experienced throughout my life, they were in a state of disbelief when they heard this news. They were not receptive to this idea. I knew that I was in God's hands and I had already purchased my airline ticket. I placed my trust in the Lord.

The following day, I returned to Tahsis. From Lethbridge to Calgary, and Calgary to Vancouver, the flights were unremarkable. When we boarded the plane to travel to Campbell River, the pilot told the passengers to expect turbulent conditions. A short time after liftoff, the pilot announced that the plane might be diverted to Nanaimo due to the turbulence. Midway to Campbell River, I looked out of the plane window. A large, loosely formed white ball was moving towards the plane. When it hit us, the plane shook with the insult of the impact. Everyone screamed.

"If you want me to get to Africa, you need to land this plane safely now," I cried out to God, and He brought us back to the ground.

My first trip to Nairobi, Kenya, began March 30, 1996. I remained in Africa until September 5. Two weeks after celebrating my seventy-first birthday, my life-long dream was being fulfilled. God was true to His promise. I needed to be patient and wait for His timing. I was moved by God's faithfulness.

When I first landed in Nairobi, I had the most awesome feeling. The intense feeling caught me by surprise. I felt as if I was coming home at last and asked God, "Why is this feeling so powerful and so consuming?"

He told me, "You have supported missions; you have prayed for missionaries; and you have advised mission workers when they asked you what to do in their situations. Your spirit has been in Africa all of these years. The feeling you have is coming from your spirit."

From Nairobi, I was scheduled to fly in a small mission plane to Watza, Zaire. Zaire is located in central Africa, near the equator.

When I was at the border, officials surveyed my suitcase and its contents. The ruling was strict and prohibitive. A surcharge of $100 in U.S. funds was applied for each electrical unit, and I was carrying four. The officials saw my omni-chord and asked with interest, "What is this?"

"It's my musical instrument," I replied.

"Play for us, sing," they told me.

"Only if you are good to me," I responded boldly. "I am here to help the poor people. I do not want to leave all of my money here at the border."

"Just sing and play," they said.

So I responded by singing four verses of a song that God gave me.

> *Do you know Jesus loves you?*
> *Do you know he died for you?*
> *Whoever you may be, wherever you may go,*
> *You can know that He loves you.*

I looked up to see the officials clapping and dancing in my midst. God helped me once again. I paid $10 and entered the country, but while I had been singing, I noticed a missionary standing on the other side of the border. It was obvious to me that he was watching intently and praying from behind his hands.

From the border, I made my way to Watza where Mr. and Mrs. Graves met me at the airport. My introduction to Watza was extra special. As we proceeded by car down the street, I noticed people lining both sides of the road. They waved and shouted pleasantries. It was a royal welcome and I felt like royalty indeed.

I lived with Mr. and Mrs. Graves for the first two months. While in Watza, I prepared over 1,000 books for the mission library. Mr. Graves made the labels on a computer and I matched the labels to the books. Since the books were written in

French and I was not familiar with the language, we completed twenty books at a time.

Once a week, Mrs. Graves held meetings in their home. The women who attended also attended the mission church. I spoke to them about the gospel and Mrs. Graves translated my message into French.

Also, I had the opportunity to teach English to two men from the church. I was surprised that they showed an interest in learning English because French was the language taught in school.

When Mr. and Mrs. Graves went to the garden to prepare the Sunday service and to spend some time in sanctuary, I remained back at the mission. I sang for the workers as the poor lined up to get food.

Near the conclusion of my first visit to Africa, Mr. and Mrs. Graves took me on a short holiday. We visited a nearby mission where all of the missionaries were from Germany. I was so surprised to be in the midst of German speaking people in Africa. While resting and finding some solitude, I painted a picture of Africa.

I returned by plane to Nairobi and worked at YWAM for the next three months. The man and woman who ran the feeding centre there provided my lodging. Twice a week, children came to clean up in the shower facilities located there. Once the children were refreshed they participated in a sing-along. A Bible lesson was presented before the food was served. I helped with the singing and provided the majority of the Bible lessons. Once clean and nourished, the children returned to what they knew to be home, and I returned to my time of prayer.

When I was not participating in activities at the feeding centre, I made school visits within the community. I was pleased to find so many of the schools open. The teachers welcomed me into their classrooms and I taught the children about Jesus.

Prior to my visit to Africa, I had made puppets. The children responded to these puppets and demonstrated such excitement.

It was great fun to see their smiling faces so full of glee and amusement.

I found it interesting to discover that I experienced greater freedom to share the gospel in Nairobi, Kenya, than in Winnipeg, Canada. My ministry was met with openness on the street and in the classroom. Back in Canada, so many rules and regulations pertaining to human rights limit our freedom to share the gospel.

My street outreach was a major part of my ministry in Nairobi. I carried my omni-chord and walked the streets. One day, I was asked to travel to an area in the Kibera Slums where I had never been before. I was told that the people in that area were unfamiliar with people who have white skin.

"Prepare yourself," I was told, "for they may react to the colour of your skin."

I saw children when we arrived, and when they saw me they screamed and ran away. It was true, they had never seen a white person before. I started to sing and the children stopped running and turned back to see what was happening. I continued to sing and they slowly, but cautiously, approached me to take a closer look. It was with that instrument, my omni-chord, that I was able to get close to many children. It turned out to be a bridge of love for them to cross over.

My puppets were close at hand as well, and I was ready to sing and provide the message of Jesus as the children gathered around me. The puppet shows intrigued them but drew the adults to the inner circle as well. The people told me that they had never seen puppets like mine, except on television. They appreciated the puppet shows that taught them about Jesus. When I asked them if they would like to sing, it was obvious by their facial expressions that they welcomed the opportunity.

On September 5, it was time to leave Nairobi. I was very grateful to God for giving me the opportunity to minister in Africa. The moments had been so very rewarding. Many children, and many adults as well, came to accept Jesus during my stay. Three marriages were saved following counselling sessions with the couples. I helped them understand their marriage commitment in the eyes of God. I had experienced difficulties in my own marital relationship and was able to understand the situations the couples described to me. I was able to empathize and support them.

The hardships that I had experienced in marriage were of value to me in Africa. I told God how much I appreciated those hardships in my life so that I could be of service to the couples in Africa.

Before my departure from Africa, I was asked, "Will you return to Kenya?"

I responded simply, "God willing!"

I settled back into my home in Tahsis but it was not long before I realized I would have to sell it and find a more suitable place to live. The necessary conveniences were situated at such a distance from my home that I would have to depend on others for transportation and to get my needs met. During the fall months, I moved to Campbell River. Many people from my church offered their assistance and simplified what could have been an onerous task. I was grateful to God that he prompted so many to come along beside me.

In December, I received a phone call from Mr. and Mrs. Graves. They had returned to Canada because there was an uprising where they were in Africa and they were forced to run for their lives. They hired someone they knew who owned a boat to take them across the lake and make their escape.

Once settled in Campbell River, I learned about travel arrangements for a return trip to Kenya. In February, I contacted Mennonite Travel, which offers reduced rates for missionaries serving abroad. In short order, my travel plans were in place.

I made my second trip to Africa on March 21, 1997. In Canada, March 21 represented the dawning of spring. In contrast, this time of year in Nairobi marked a much cooler season. In addition to it being winter, Nairobi is located at a higher altitude, which promotes cooler air patterns.

Many people have asked me, "Isn't it hot there in Nairobi?" I was able to inform these people that the altitude is over one mile so even though Nairobi is situated close to the equator, the altitude contributes to a cooler climate.

I returned to YWAM and reunited with the same couple that had provided my lodging the previous year. It felt right to be back on African soil.

I attended a church named "The Door". Prayer meetings were held once per week in the morning. At one of the prayer meetings, I noticed a woman sitting with her head bowed. She was crying out to God. In this church, people prayed individually with little interaction with others. I moved and sat beside the woman and prayed with her and invited her to come with me to my place. Once there, we shared breakfast and fellowship together. She left with a loaf of bread as a blessing.

Later, this woman told me that on the way to prayer, she told God that she did not have any food and had asked God to provide a loaf of bread for that day.

God provided for her needs.

The Lord's Prayer says, "Give us this day our daily bread." God wants us to look to Him for our provision. He cares about the details of our lives each and every day.

The woman I had met at prayer that morning accompanied me to the streets where I did my outreach ministry. The breakfast we shared and our prayers before God brought us closer than we had expected. I came to know this woman on a very personal level. I realized that she had a heart for giving to others but her own resources were very limited.

At the YWAM mission, the woman in charge attended to the food at the feeding centre. My contribution was to minister to the children when they came to the centre for food. Two times per week, I was able to care for them and minister to their needs in an environment that was safe and nurturing. I shared Bible lessons, songs and prayers with them. Many of these children found it difficult to understand what we were teaching because they were hungry.

Sadly, many young girls reported that they were given to men for a night. In turn, their mothers received money. The girls were placed in situations that were unsafe and unfamiliar to them. The girls were shocked when they were taken away from their homes. Innocent girls had no idea what they were moving into when they walked away into the night, unprepared for the abuse they would endure at the hands of these men.

The stories related by these young girls were heartbreaking. How was a young girl supposed to understand that her mother sent her off into the night with a stranger so that the family could receive money for survival? How was a young girl supposed to develop a loving relationship with her mother after being subjected to such horrific experiences? How was a young girl able to learn a different path in life for herself and the daughters she would have in the future?

In response to the heartbreaking stories, we at the feeding centre were prompted to teach the children better ways to earn money for their families, like how to make jewellery. The children were given an alternative so they could provide for their families without losing their innocence and their dignity. They were given opportunities to sell their crafts under the supervision of adults who would watch out for their welfare.

The road leading to the city centre was about a third of a mile from the mission. While walking along this road one day, I passed by a garbage heap. The stench was so powerful that I was forced to turn my head the other way. As I continued, I thought I heard something and turned to look at the pile of garbage. There, I saw a young girl about five years old sitting on top of the heap eating a rotten orange. I was mortified!

I collected my personal resources and bought baking supplies, made homemade pancakes and added raisins to make them more nutritious. The next day when I arrived at the garbage heap, I was prepared to offer homemade food to the girl and other children there. The expressions on their faces were worth more than gold.

Another day, while en route to the city, a gentleman and I came across a young man sprawled across the road. He had been glue sniffing. We asked him why he was lying in the middle of the road and he confessed that he was too hungry to go on and that he just wanted to end it all. We encouraged him to get off the road and told him that we were planning to provide a feeding centre close by. "Hold on!" we implored.

Three days later, on June 26, 1997, the feeding centre opened at the Assembly of God Mission. God responded to this need very quickly. He heard our prayers and He made a way. Praise God for his prompt response!

The stench of that garbage heap was not only overpowering for me, but also lethal. I developed an allergic reaction to the odors. Close to 100 blisters formed all over my body. They were very painful but if I broke them open, the pain subsided over time. In order to avoid the exposure of the polluted environment, I asked the children to come to the feeding centre.

The feeding centre at the Assembly of God Mission was my first in Africa. My days and nights were full of activity for the Lord. I worked at the feeding centre,x continued my contribution at the YWAM mission and pursued my outreach ministry in the streets. On Sundays, I taught a youth class at The Door. I really enjoyed my time with these young people. They were very receptive to learning the word of God as I read it to them. But they seemed alarmed to hear of God's expectations, such as what the Bible says about morality, sinfulness, stealing, deception, and so on. Bible reading was followed by questions and discussion.

Operating a feeding centre presented many challenges. It was a safe environment so the children liked to come to play while they waited for their meal but they needed supervision to prevent fights from breaking out. Cooperative play needed to be fostered because they were not accustomed to playing with each other.

Local individuals came to the centre to volunteer. They wanted to serve the food and were believers, but they were not experienced with the routines. They required much teaching about the tasks assigned to them, needing direction and more redirection until they learned to work together cooperatively. If they were not willing to follow instructions, they were asked to leave the centre.

The children learned that they had to arrive at the feeding centre early enough to clean up their physical bodies. They washed up at the baptismal tank located outside the centre. Once clean and refreshed, they were allowed to enter the dining hall. Each morning, songs and Bible lessons preceded the food. God came first. The Lord was praised with worship and thanksgiving and the children learned to follow the routines. Any who chose to be disobedient were turned away. In the end, they abided by the rules outlined for them. It was a clear illustration of how children need to have boundaries so that they know what is expected and what is acceptable behaviour.

Midway through my visit to Africa, I felt the need for some time away to restore my energies. I made arrangements with the couple who ran the mission to stay at the guest house for the coming weekend. My schedule was so busy that my weekend arrived in what seemed like no time at all.

As I walked up the steps to the guest house, I was so pleased to see Mr. Graves standing on the front porch. He was deep in thought, trying to determine how he could get in touch with me. Just as I was surprised to see him, he was equally surprised to see me approaching. God brought Mr. and Mrs. Graves to the guest house at the very time that I travelled there for a rest. We had a wonderful time of sharing and fellowship.

Mr. and Mrs. Graves informed me that they had been reassigned to Kisumo, which was located very close to Victoria

Falls. They invited me to join their service there but I declined, explaining that I was very busy participating at the feeding centres and conducting my street outreach ministry.

As I had planned, I made arrangements to leave Nairobi September 7. I informed the couple at YWAM that I would not be returning to work with them at that mission. I told the cook at the Assembly of God Mission feeding centre that I would return if I was directed by God to do so. Until I knew more information, I would send funds on a monthly basis to help support the feeding centre. With that, I left Africa for the second time.

I spent the winter months in Campbell River, British Columbia. The local church was very supportive. The pastor had a television broadcast and on several occasions, he invited me to join him and share information about my work in Africa. The community became aware of my mission work through these broadcasts and people offered donations in support of what I was doing.

Sometime after the Christmas holiday, the local newspaper wrote an article about my work in Africa, which was a real blessing because it opened a door into one of the community businesses. I was given permission to sit in front of one of the stores and sing to the Lord. While I shared my music with the community, many people offered donations for my work in Africa.

Springtime marked the season of my third trip to Africa. I departed on March 26, 1998. Shortly after my seventy-third birthday, I stood again on African soil. Upon arrival in Nairobi, I resumed my work with the Assembly of God Mission. My efforts were more concentrated because I was able to attend on a daily basis.

The African Inland Mission (AIM) gave me permission to place a donation box in their guest house, where individuals could leave money to support my feeding ministry. Self-made information booklets were available at a minimal cost to promote the Lord's message and explain my outreach ministry.

The feeding centres and teaching of the gospel continued as in the previous year. I took some photographs of the centres and the work being done and organized them on a poster board. The display attracted individuals to me and allowed me an opportunity to expound upon the work being accomplished. Many people asked questions and responded to the information they heard. I was often asked to keep talking about the mission work.

One day, while sharing my mission stories, a young boy told me, "Your money is gone from your purse."

I brought my purse to the front of my body to check it and, sure enough, the money was gone—1,000 Kenyan shillings had been lifted. This money was allocated for the feeding centre to purchase the needed food supplies for the coming week. I was shocked and felt numb. It was like taking food out of children's mouths, and a child was responsible for stealing it.

Meanwhile, I returned to AIM to find out if there was any money in the donation box. While I was in the guest house, a stranger approached and pointed at me.

"As the widow's oil did not run dry, so you will always have food for your orphans," he declared.

The word spread throughout the community that someone had taken money from the elderly woman conducting street ministry. Before the sun set that day, I received more than three times the amount that had been stolen from my purse.

The following day, I shared the incident with a group of children and praised God for His faithfulness. I used the incident as an opportunity to teach the children that stealing does not benefit us. One of them reported that the young boy who stole the money broke his leg while he was running away from the scene.

"God rewards those who serve the Lord," I explained. "God provides for those who do His work. He remains faithful. We can count on Him."

The children were excited to realize how God works in our lives. The devil intended this incident for evil purposes but God used it as an opportunity to promote His goodness. The children were moved by the way that God demonstrated his faithfulness and they learned a lesson about the goodness of God's love. It was a lesson that they would never forget.

Shortly after the robbery, I was invited to a fellow Christian's home. There, I met Pastor Simon, who lived in a place called Kissie. He and I shared stories about our community work. He was working with the poor children in his community as well. I invited Pastor Simon to join me in Nairobi where he could participate in my growing ministry. He told me that he would let me know of his decision after a time of prayer.

Before long, Pastor Simon joined me in Nairobi. He and I kept busy planning and working together. Our plan was to register the ministry. In June, 1998, it was accomplished. We registered The Overcomers' Caring Ministries officially. On June 26, we celebrated the first anniversary of the feeding centre at the Assembly of God Mission.

One day, Pastor Simon made a request. We were conversing about our plans when he asked if I could remain at the centre because he had to go to meet with his father. I informed him that I had some shopping to do but when I returned he could go. I departed on my shopping trip a few minutes later.

While I was in the store shopping, it seemed that I encountered one obstacle after another. Either I could not find the items I needed or they were not available. I appealed to other shoppers to help me but no one I approached seemed to speak English. Every turn seemed to present another delay. For some reason, I sensed that God wanted me to relax and not hurry through the experience. Something just seemed to be wrong. Finally, I had completed my shopping and was ready to return to the centre.

Pastor Simon was watching out the window when I arrived back at the feeding centre. Upon seeing me, he ran out and shouted a hasty farewell and travelled by bus to the embassy. At the very time he was heading to his destination, the embassy was attacked and there was a large explosion. He arrived to find many people injured and many others who needed to be transported to hospital. He remained in the vicinity to help out in whatever way he could.

Later, he learned that his father had missed the bus to the embassy. Thankfully, he had not been present when the explosion occurred.

Pastor Simon arrived back at the centre very late that night. When we spoke about the events of the day, it became apparent to us that God had intervened in a most helpful way. We realized why He had lengthened my shopping trip. If Pastor Simon had left sooner, he would have been at the embassy when the attack took place. God nudged me to take my time and protected both Pastor Simon and his father.

What a wonderful Father we have. When we trust and obey, the Lord works wonders in our lives.

Following the explosion at the embassy, Pastor Simon returned to his home, on the outskirts of Kissie to check on his family. A church conference was planned for over the weekend. The guest speakers scheduled for the event were Americans. They were advised not to attend the conference. Pastor Simon and I were invited to speak in their place.

When the conference was ready to begin, Pastor Simon had not returned from his trip to visit his family. I was left to do the speaking engagement on my own. I was confident because the Lord placed a very special topic in my heart—learning about the Lord and developing a close relationship with Him.

I began by saying that many people in Kenya are brought to the Lord. The people are "born again". However, following this, there is a great void. Christian brothers and sisters must take responsibility and lead the new believers in the faith, I said.

After welcoming the Lord into their hearts, the people in Kenya were not taught how to grow up in the Lord. They were not taught the blessed assurance. They were not given instruction about the importance of daily devotions and daily communication with the Lord.

I talked about how, in my experience, people had been "born again" but were not fed the necessary direction for developing fellowship with the Lord. I shared with the audience the importance of walking in the light. Fellow believers are required to lead by example.

Further, I informed the audience that many individuals had problems reading and their reading difficulties interfered with their ability to read the word. They required assistance from fellow believers more advanced in their faith.

After the conference, Pastor Simon and I returned to Nairobi to work at the Assembly of God Mission feeding centre. We met with some resistance upon our arrival. The people at the Assembly of God wanted me to work with them but did not extend the same invitation to Pastor Simon. They were convinced that he would lead me away from their organization. From the onset, they were not receptive to opening the door to him. I was caught in a very uncomfortable position. The Lord gave me a vision that instructed me on what to do next.

In my vision, I was standing with my feet firmly planted on the ground. I was outside the feeding centre, standing in the middle of the compound yard. I heard the voices of children calling to me. "We are hungry too."

The vision helped me to realize that God was leading me away from the Assembly of God Mission. I returned home to Canada a short time later. I knew God had put time and distance between me and the predicament at the mission.

Back in Campbell River, I learned that some doors were closing. My opportunity to sing in front of the storefronts was discontinued. Potential customers voiced their complaints and my time to sing to the Lord was abbreviated but my focus was shifted elsewhere. I was directed to an office called "Birth Right".

I participated in activities aimed at helping young people make appropriate decisions about pregnancy. Together with other staff members, we showed movies, demonstrated outcomes using diagrams, and provided information to these young women. We talked with the women who were considering abortion. We aimed to equip these individuals so that they would be well informed about the decisions they were making.

In 1999, I returned to Africa. Shortly after my arrival on April 6, I learned that Pastor Simon had plans to be married. In Africa, the groom pays for the wedding, all related wedding expenses, and provides the bride's family with a dowry. The dowry is based on the education of the prospective bride.

Since Pastor Simon was working with me, I was obliged to help out in whatever way I could. I made the wedding dress, the veil, the flower arrangements and the wedding cake. Without my contributions, Pastor Simon would have been forced to leave the community work that we were doing and secure a job to pay for the expenses of the wedding. The wedding was held on July 31.

In Africa, it was customary to have two messages at the marriage. The first message was about accepting Jesus as your Lord and Saviour. The second was directed to the bride and groom about having a home. When the couple exchanged wedding rings, they held their hands up high so that everyone in the congregation could see them putting the rings on each other's fingers. Following the rings, the couple exchanged their vows and then a feast followed the ceremony.

Pastor Simon and his new wife, Eunice, made their first home close to The Door.

Eight

A Miracle at Home

In the early part of 2000, the pastors in the Campbell River area received information about two men who were anointed by God. The two men were known as the Suttera twins, and were given special gifting by God to counsel others. These men had travelled to various points in the world where God led them to conduct revival meetings. They alerted our pastors of their plans to visit Campbell River and provided teaching materials that could be used to train counsellors prior to their arrival.

Representatives of the area churches gathered together and reviewed the appropriateness of the training materials. I participated in these meetings and completed the counsellor training myself.

When the twins arrived, people were invited to attend one of the revival meetings, which continued over several weeks. They gave the people an opportunity to hear the gospel, to pray and to receive counselling.

After many evenings of counselling, we counsellors were instructed to take a full Wednesday, both day and night, to rest and relax in the Lord. We were told to avoid phone calls and any counselling during that period. I took the time to relax all day. Late in the afternoon, I started to plan for my evening meal. Simultaneously, there was a knock on the door just as the phone began to ring. I answered the door and asked the woman to wait while I answered my phone.

The woman on the phone indicated that she needed to see me. She told me that she needed to prepare her dinner first, but she could be available to meet with me in about two hours. I agreed to meet with her later, then returned to the woman waiting on my doorstep. She informed me that she needed my help. She said that she was there to take me out for dinner. She thought that we could talk while we enjoyed a meal together. I accompanied this woman to the restaurant where she described her situation. We discussed her problem and I offered direction. She informed me that my guidance was helpful before taking me back to my home, just in time to invite the other woman in for a time of sharing. The second woman described her concerns and we entered into prayer and fellowship. She later thanked me for my help as I saw her to the door.

I went to bed that night, knowing that I had not followed the guidelines set out for counsellors, but I felt in my heart that I had observed what God had set out for me to do. I went to sleep at peace with my choices.

The following morning, I took some reading materials from the shelf. As I started to read, I realized I was not wearing my glasses. I continued to read and then, with great joy in my spirit, I got up from my bed and walked to the bedroom window to look out at the day.

After 68 years of total reliance on prescription lenses, God had touched my eyes. At 75 years of age, I was able to read without my glasses. I did not need them any longer. I looked out at the world with a new vision. Praise God for all that He has done!

I went to church and shared the miracle of my restored vision. I laughed and I cried as I thanked the Lord for His blessings. God returned my eyesight. Praise God for His wondrous works.

Nine

Nesting in Nairobi

Everyone in Canada told me that I was too old to return to Africa at 75 years of age. Medical insurance costs were very high. I turned to the Lord and asked, "Lord, what do you say?"
He told me, "I'm not finished with you yet."
Nairobi welcomed me back on April 3, 2000. Pastor Simon and Eunice were there to greet me when I arrived. They were surprised to see that I was not wearing glasses.
We travelled to Kissie. There, I was introduced to four young orphans, who were in Pastor Simon's care. We brought them back with us and rented a room nearby for them to call home. One of the orphans was named Herbert. He was older and he cared for the younger ones. Pastor Simon, Eunice, and I shared a home.
I was also introduced to some of the little-known aspects of church life in Africa. For example, once a year, an EXPO was held as a fundraiser for the various feeding centres, with individual centres each setting up their tables. They sold various wares that could be used at other centres. I made some puppets and some banners with gospel messages to sell at the EXPO. Each

feeding centre managed the funds collected at their table and applied the earnings to their particular needs. This event was a big attraction for the people in the city of Nairobi.

Some churches rented space from schools for their Sunday service. Prayer meetings were held in family homes. When a baptism ceremony was held, it often took place in the community swimming pool, which was rented by the church for the event. Our church had a baptism ceremony while I was in Africa.

It was difficult to coordinate a baptism ceremony with the community using the pool. In addition to the problem of availability, sometimes the pool was not readily accessible and, therefore, limited the number of people who could attend.

One Sunday, I met a man named Meshach at church. Meshach became our choir director. We made a tape recording of our choir singing to the Lord. I enjoyed being a part of the choir. Praise and worship music was good for the spirit.

Pastor Simon also introduced me to a woman who operated a business in the uptown section of Nairobi. Doreen and her husband were very wealthy. Doreen's husband was one of 200 government officials in Kenya. One evening, Pastor Simon, Eunice and I were invited to Doreen's home for dinner. While the maid served a delicious African meal, we discussed the outreach ministry and the needs of people in Kenya.

During my stay, I learned that Pastor Simon and Eunice were starting a family. Almost a year after their marriage, Simon and Eunice were blessed with a son, whom they named Joshua.

When African babies are born, the skin pigment is light. Within two to three weeks, it becomes darker. When a baby is born in the hospital, the mother and baby are not released to go home until the hospital bill is paid in full. It is quite a challenge to collect 58,000 Kenyan shillings. In Canadian currency, that is about $1,000. The longer the stay in hospital, the greater the bill becomes.

I paid their hospital bill and Doreen provided the car to bring Eunice and the baby home.

I was scheduled to leave Kenya on August 30. One Sunday, a short time before my departure, I was invited to preach at the church I was attending. That particular Sunday, Pastor Simon's brother, Bernard, was visiting Nairobi. After the church service, Bernard told me that I was a good evangelist. He invited me to come and speak to the congregation at his home church in Kissie. His invitation was declined because I was leaving to return to Canada on that day. I instructed Bernard that he needed to live his faith and he needed to pray for any unsaved relatives.

Upon my return to Campbell River I was challenged by my limited finances. To augment my income, I picked blackberries and sold them to the seniors who lived in the trailer court. One woman gave me a large fish in trade for a pail of blackberries. It was a beneficial and delicious trade.

I attended the Vineyard Church each Sunday morning. Sunday evening, I caught a ride to a different church. During the week, I attended the prayer meeting at the Vineyard. The people who attended Vineyard Church were very supportive of my mission work in Africa.

One day, I was contacted by a woman who had worked with me at Birth Right. She invited me to visit her church and speak about my experiences in Africa. The church was located on a small island off the coast of Vancouver Island. We travelled there by ferry and I shared my stories of work in the mission field and at the feeding centres, emphasizing the ways the Lord had blessed me in preparation for my experiences in Africa. I related how the Lord used all of my former life experiences to the fullest in my missionary work. The members of the church blessed me with donations for my African mission outreach.

I travelled to Africa May 1, 2001. I planned to stay in Kenya for three months and return to Canada August 2. When I arrived, Pastor Simon reported that he had been investigating appropriate real estate for our mission work and drove me to see a plot of land located toward the outskirts of Nairobi. We viewed the property together and discussed the possibilities of ownership.

There were conditions to consider before making our decision. If we purchased the property, we would be required to build a wall. The structure would have to be sufficient to prevent intruders from seeing into the area or entering from beyond the wall.

After careful consideration, we agreed to purchase the plot of land at a cost of 1,000 Kenyan shillings. We constructed a wall of iron sheeting at the peripheral borders to a height of eight feet. Once the wall was constructed, we shifted our attention to our outreach work. Further developments at the site would have to be planned, so they were tabled for later discussion.

I continuously wrote prayer letters to request support for the mission work I was doing in Africa. In response to one of my letters, I received a phone call from a woman named Donna. Donna indicated that she was interested in working with children in Africa and arrangements were made over the phone to have her come and visit me in my home. After several days of fellowship together, Donna decided to come to Africa.

She arrived after I was already settled and was anxious to make a contribution. A number of suggestions were outlined for her. Initially, she was asked to catalogue the books in the library and she completed that task. Next, she was invited to accompany us while we did our outreach work.

Donna was not prepared for the poverty that surrounded us in the streets of Nairobi. She became overwhelmed by the magnitude of the needs of the people who lived there and after only a couple of visits to the streets, she was not able to continue the outreach work. She became emotional and chose to stay at the house. Pastor Simon and I continued to do our outreach ministry but Donna occupied her time by writing letters to Canada, and was evasive about their contents. Unfortunately, her assessment of the work that Pastor Simon and I were doing did not meet with her expectations. She described our outreach in a negative light and made accusations about Pastor Simon.

Donna and I returned to Canada on August 2, 2001 but, as a result of her observations and her critical assessment of our outreach ministry, Pastor Simon was investigated by an impartial mission representative. The accusations made against him were unfounded and he was completely cleared of any wrongdoing.

Upon reflection, it was clear that Donna's interference created lasting obstacles. Her criticisms served to unravel work that had taken much time and energy to put into place. Even though Pastor Simon had been vindicated of any accusations brought against him, the church was no longer willing to support the mission work.

I travelled to Winnipeg in September, 2001, and remained on the prairies through the month of October. While visiting in Winnipeg, I was able to generate financial support from a number of churches. It was clear, however, that the damage that was done to the support network would require the intervention of God in order to amass the necessary funds.

Usually, I made my travel arrangements very early in January. Due to the investigation of Pastor Simon, I was not able to finalize my plans until well into February and the delay affected my choice of flights to Africa.

In the past, I had flown through the Netherlands or through England. This time, those routes were not available to me and I had to travel through Arabia. As well, I was forced to change planes in two different places along the way. The second connection was the most uncomfortable. I sensed a spirit that was truly foreign to me. Even though the airport itself was beautiful in design and color, I made up my mind that I never wanted to travel through that location again.

In all of my travels to Africa, this was the first time I experienced any problems with my luggage, which was left behind in Arabia. Fortunately, it arrived safely, a few days after I landed in Africa.

Prior to my arrival in Nairobi on May 1, 2002, an election had been held in December. Following the election, there was a great uprising. People from the slum area left their homes and found refuge within our compound and settled inside of the walls of our tract of land. It was an empty space, void of any buildings. Fortunately, Pastor Simon had provided a key to the compound to a man who managed things in that area. The man was able to let the people enter the compound and find safety. The outer wall was made of sheet metal so the rebels were not able to see inside. The people who sought refuge were kept safe within the walls.

From that time forward, the people who found safety within those walls were very grateful and showed appreciation to us for saving their lives. Our act of kindness opened doors for us to teach the gospel in the area, driving the open practice of witchcraft away.

Unfortunately, the people who moved into the compound lost everything from their homes. God gave them a place of refuge in the political storm and saved their lives and provided shelter when it was needed.

An area close to where Pastor Simon lived was named Toy. It had an open market where people could buy food and wares at reasonable prices. Everything was out in the open and exposed to the elements. Some merchants were able to erect umbrellas over their tables in order to protect themselves from the sun, but it was the openness of the market that contributed to the lower prices.

I remained in Africa until August 3. During my stay, Pastor Simon spent a great deal of time with the authorities making arrangements and collecting the papers necessary to get water to our project site. The fees were paid and then we waited lengthy periods of time before receiving the associated paperwork.

When some of the papers were not received, Pastor Simon returned to the authorities for an explanation. He was informed that the administrators, who controlled the water supply, had changed and there were different individuals in place. Subsequently, we paid a second time for the same paperwork.

Trenches were dug and pipes were installed. The water supply was functional but not available at all times, and the system was not completed. As a result, a worker needed to be in place to put the water into containers as it flowed into the compound.

At about the same time, the local school board cancelled the leasing agreement for the Sunday services held at the school because someone had acted inappropriately there. Apparently words were exchanged and the individual spoke on behalf of the church. This error in judgment cost the church its place of worship.

In response, Pastor Simon and I found and purchased a tract of land close to Toy and a new church was built on the site. Pastor Simon found an old pulpit in need of repair so I prepared a small banner to hang on the front, which read: "Lord, speak to me. I will listen and obey."

I held afternoon meetings with the women of the church once per week in various homes and taught lessons about marriage relationships. We discussed relationship building with husbands and about the outcomes of divorce, about non-Christians, about submitting, and about prayer. The Lord led me to encourage these women to find prayer sisters. If they acted as prayer sisters, they could support each other and be open and truthful about their needs.

While I was staying with Pastor Simon, Eunice and Joshua, we did not have much food to eat. Joshua, by this time, was an active two year old, who kept Eunice hopping. God gave me the following verse: "Trust in the Lord and feed on His faithfulness."

Another version of this scripture reads:

"Trust in the Lord and do good. Then you will live in the land and enjoy its food. Find your delight in the Lord. Then he will give you everything your heart really wants" (Psalm 37:3, 4).

A group of twenty pastors from Kissie and churches in Nairobi, gathered at our church for a time of praise and worship. I had received instruction about praise and worship previously, so I led the group in a time of fellowship and song. I explained to the group that we cannot enter the Holy of Holies with sin in our hearts. Before we lead praise and worship in the spirit, our sins must be cleansed.

On Sundays, I led the praise and worship time in our church. African people love to praise God and put all of themselves into it. My messages directed them to move beyond the cleansing and into the Holy of Holies. I continued to focus on the message of growth in Jesus Christ.

When I first travelled to Africa, it was apparent to me that pastors needed to place attention on bringing up the saved, "the born again", in Christ. People became "born again" and then were left without proper teaching. The pastors needed to direct the spiritual growth of Christ in Christian fellowship. I prayed for five years about this concern. I asked the Lord to bring someone to the pastors in Africa who would develop this teaching. I prayed that the pastors would learn to respond to the needs of their flock.

Finally, in 2002, my prayers were answered. Two conferences were held in Nairobi during the summer months. As requested, the teaching focussed on bringing up Christians in the Lord and I was invited to attend. Conference presenters shared information about building spiritual relationships with the Lord. They emphasized that pastors needed to help Christians grow in their spiritual walk. I was very grateful to God for answering my prayers once more.

On my last Sunday in Nairobi, I was invited to speak at the church. I spoke about the adorning of the bride of Christ. I shared that we are called to be clothed with humility, and with a quiet and submissive spirit. The Holy Spirit moved in the hearts of the people that day. Many couples were not able to sleep that night. Instead, they confessed to each other and opened their hearts, as they pledged to work together in unity.

I left Nairobi and my heart was encouraged by the moving of the Holy Spirit in the hearts of the people.

Once more back home in Campbell River, Pastor Simon sent word that there had been a significant upheaval in Nairobi. He advised against me travelling to Africa that year; it would not be safe for me to visit due to the unrest. I accepted his wisdom and did not go to Nairobi in 2003, but sent money to support the ongoing work.

In the meantime, I became very involved in Birth Right and regular church activities. In addition, I had to sell my belongings because I had decided to move to Winnipeg in the spring of 2004.

In the trailer court where I lived, a woman was experiencing emotional problems. Her psychiatrist had recommended she purchase a musical instrument because he believed that music would be very therapeutic for her, and I needed to sell my organ.

It was interesting to me that God worked this out so well. Just at the time that I had an organ for sale, this woman was looking for a musical instrument. The woman came to my home and purchased it, and when she came, she accepted the Lord into her heart on that day and expressed her gratitude to me for witnessing to her. In my heart, the music played on.

About a month before I was scheduled to move to Winnipeg, I had an accident. I entered a store but did not notice that the floor was wet and fell down on the slippery surface. As a result of the fall, I broke my right wrist and hurt my hip as well, but my wrist had broken the fall, which saved me from a broken hip. The store proprietors were attentive to my needs and paid for all the costs incurred in travelling to and from the hospital, and paid me $7,500. I used $500 for personal expenses and the remainder was directed to Africa.

As a result of my accident, I did not have sufficient help to prepare for the move. I sold most of my belongings and shipped the rest of my possessions by bus. Friends were at the Winnipeg bus depot to meet me and welcome me into their home.

Ten

My Adventure Continues

I left for Africa on April 29, 2004, and planned to stay there until August 4. Pastor Simon and his family welcomed me into their home. Shortly after my arrival, we drove to the project site, which was the focus of this particular trip. I had drawn plans for it but was discouraged from visiting it during construction. Pastor Simon advised me that once the labourers saw my white face, they would raise the prices. The building commenced.

I provided the funding for the project but I did not see the progress. I relied on the feedback given by Pastor Simon. Three rooms were constructed along one wall. These areas were designated as space for the feeding centre.

I resumed my outreach ministry activities in Nairobi and preached every Sunday in Pastor Simon's church and was invited to preach in other churches as well. One Sunday, I preached in three different churches. God gave his grace.

My preaching drew attention to the words written on the banner that hung from the front of the pulpit—"Lord, speak to me. I will listen and obey"—so I made a similar small sign to use when I preached at other churches in the area, to serve as a visual aid while I presented the message. I was able to speak from my heart because I knew the message applied to me as well. God always gave me the message He wanted me to convey. The feedback I received from the people confirmed that the message was from God. The people received exactly what they needed to hear.

The last Sunday that I was in Nairobi, we travelled to the feeding centre after the morning church service had concluded. We held an opening ceremony to introduce the feeding centre to the neighbourhood. We invited children to come and adults were encouraged to accompany them if they were available to attend. Prior to serving the food, Pastor Simon led a church service. Several adults accepted the Lord into their hearts on that special day.

We anticipated that approximately fifty children would visit the feeding centre for the opening. Instead, 200 people, mostly children, came for the ceremony. We had sufficient food in a large pot to feed fifty but it was as if the pot was bottomless. It did not empty until the last person was fed. God provided enough food. He multiplied our supply. Praise God!

In those days, the centre operated on Mondays, Wednesdays, and Fridays for the very poor children who did not attend school. It reopened on Saturdays to reach out to any children from the area who had not attended during the week.

The feeding centre also operated as an outreach. On Sundays, Pastor Simon gave a morning sermon in his church. Following the service, he retired to his home to eat a meal with his family and then he travelled to the feeding centre and gave an afternoon service.

Before I left Nairobi, I told my fellow workers that when I returned to Canada I would not have a place to live. I informed them that I would be staying with my brother at the beginning. They assured me that they would pray for me.

"You have helped us so much that God is going to give you a place very quickly," they said.

Upon arrival in Winnipeg, my brother was at the airport to pick me up. I asked him to stop where I could buy a newspaper. After searching the ads for rental accommodations, I was blessed to locate a new home within two days. I leased a one-bedroom suite at 10 Valhalla Drive. I was grateful to the Lord for providing a home so readily and was excited to let everyone in Africa know that God had answered their prayers.

It took some time for me to get established in my new home. I needed to retrieve some items that had been placed in storage until my return from Africa. I also needed to become familiar with the neighbourhood and services in the city. My transportation needs were settled once I became familiar with "Handi Transit" services. I was dependent on this service to move about in the city.

Faith Temple became my home church. In previous years when I had lived in Winnipeg, I used to help at this church in a variety of ways.

For many years, I attended the Billy Graham Telephone Ministry and had completed the counsellor training provided. When conferences came to the city, I participated as a counsellor on the floor. Later, I was a supervisor of counsellors. My son David, his wife, Anita, and their five children took the counsellor training as well. When Franklin Graham came to Winnipeg, David and his family were involved in the conference in various capacities. I was nearby, on the floor overseeing counsellors who were communicating with those individuals who came forward to accept Jesus as their Lord and Saviour.

As a counsellor, we were instructed to contact those people new to the faith and make certain that they had found a Bible-teaching church to attend. New believers were to be followed to make sure they were reading the word and receiving the assurance of salvation.

During this time, my son, David, developed cancer and once a week, he and I attended a different church where we could be taught about healing. David had a difficult time with his disease but the healing services helped draw us closer together in relationship.

My daughter, Lydia, was on disability due to a back injury she developed working as a nurse. My adoptive son, Allen, was struggling with some personal decisions. All in all, I felt led to develop closer relationships with my children. Now that I was living in the same city again, I believed our family was being given an opportunity to build our relationships with one another.

On December 11, 2004, two months shy of her 103rd birthday, my mother passed into heaven. She was well right up to one week before her death. Her heart had been racing and the doctors informed the family that the condition would take its toll on her overall health. My sisters were called to the hospital before my mother passed. When they arrived, they told mother she would see Jesus soon. My mother and my sisters started to sing together and Mother had her hands lifted to the Lord as she sang. Then her hands dropped and she was gone. I flew to Coldale for the funeral, which was a grand celebration of her life.

David drove me to the airport. On the way, he informed me that Pastor Simon had sent an email saying that he would pick me up at the airport in Nairobi. After saying my goodbyes to David, I proceeded through security. Once through, I realized that Pastor Simon had confused the date for my arrival. I needed to contact him.

Nearby, a businessman was using his cell phone. When he completed his call, I asked if he would let me call my son. I phoned David and asked him to send an email to Pastor Simon to clarify the date of my arrival. The businessman overheard my conversation and introduced himself to me and gave me his business card. He told me that he was a Christian.

March 11, 2005, I celebrated my eightieth birthday. May 17, 2005, marked my first journey to Kenya departing from Winnipeg. This trip took me first to Toronto, Ontario, and then to London, England. From London, I flew to Kenya.

When I arrived in Nairobi May 18, I was driven directly to the feeding centre. I looked over the site and was saddened to see that there had been very little development in my absence. At one point, there had been a flood. The kitchen floors were damaged significantly by the water and needed to be replaced. Pastor Simon arranged for that to be done and I gave him the money needed to purchase the appropriate supplies and pay the workmen. After the job was completed, Pastor Simon noted that the workers had made the floor look attractive but the quality of the cement mixture used was inferior. It was clear that they had skimped on the amount of cement needed.

Later, after a rainfall, the floor began to crumble and had to be replaced again. As a result of this experience, Pastor Simon purchased the materials himself. Money did not exchange hands with the workers until the job was completed to our satisfaction.

In order to level the surface of the ground at the site, earth was moved from one area to another. The newly leveled area allowed for more construction to take place.

During the first month of my stay, two classrooms, a dining room, and the office were constructed. The framing for these rooms was completed but the roofing was not done. In the outer area of the compound, two toilets and a shower were erected African style.

In 2004, Pastor Simon communicated with an organization from the United States that visited Nairobi. It provided pastoral training to prepare and qualify pastors to conduct weddings and funerals. Pastor Simon began the training in 2004 and completed it in 2005. In order to secure his ordination papers, he was required to pay for the training provided.

Pastor Simon explained to me that in Africa, many young people live together because they do not have the money to pay for the marriage or the associated dowry. I paid the costs of Pastor Simon's training and he was ordained in my presence. It was our hope that we could encourage young people to get married instead of living together. We were hopeful that Pastor Simon's involvement could help the couples avoid the dowry and help the parents of these young people to bless the marriage.

During my time in Africa, I preached at The Overcomers' Church each Sunday. In addition to speaking at Pastor Simon's church, I was invited to speak at various pastoral meetings.

Eleven

The Orphanage Opens

The last Sunday that I was in Africa marked the opening of the orphanage. Pastor Simon, his wife Eunice, and a social worker visited the homes in the Kibera Slums, in close proximity to the feeding centre. During the visits, the women were able to determine which children had the greatest need. In Africa, if a child is attending school, the family must have money because the children have to pay to go to school. These children were not considered for the orphanage.

Once the selection process was completed, fourteen children were welcomed to the orphanage and invited to sleep there. Forty-four other children were invited to come to the orphanage on a daily basis to eat and to go to school. It was a tragedy to not have sufficient space to house everyone.

Sometimes, children were caring for their grandmothers. Still, we had to turn them away. The orphanage was manned by three adults at all times. They cooked meals, taught lessons and acted in a supervisory capacity. Guidelines and rules were communicated to the children.

The children at the orphanage referred to me as "Mama

Helena". They crowded around me and held my hand. They sensed my love and wanted to draw near to me. The children appreciated the time that I spent with them.

I left Nairobi and settled into my life in Winnipeg once more. One day, I was contacted by a man named Derek, the business-man who let me use his cell phone in the airport. Derek asked to see me and told me he had been very inspired by our conversation at the airport. He informed me that he wanted to make a donation to the orphanage.

"You have helped me more than I am helping you," he said. "My work has been just work," he explained. "God has shown me that my work needs to be an outreach to the people."

Derek obeyed the direction initiated by God. He started a mission named Twelve Pillars, which focussed on serving aboriginal people in Winnipeg.

While home in Winnipeg, I attended a mission conference. At this conference, a representative from an international organization presented information about a mission in Nairobi.

I left Winnipeg June 13, 2006. Since I was getting older, I was planning to find an organization to assume responsibility for the orphanage. When I arrived in Nairobi, I made arrangements to visit a different mission. I learned that the mission church held a Sunday morning service led by the pastor and that the pastor's wife led a prayer meeting and directed a class for new believers.

When I arrived, they were building a room onto the side of the building designed for church activities. From this area, food was distributed at noon, three times per week. Children came there to eat a meal. The gospel was not introduced due to a perceived shortage of time. I was not pleased that the church had not done anything to promote God in the feeding centre so I decided to introduce some changes that would bring glorification to God. I purchased five, four by eight-foot sheets of plywood and painted gospel messages on them. They served as the inner walls on three sides of the building. When the children came to eat a meal, they could see that God was providing for their needs. On the walls, I had painted: "Holy, Holy, Holy are you Lord! We love and adore you."

In the background, I painted a cross with white angels all about. I also painted many hands that were raised up to worship God. I showed the children my hands, the cook's hands, and their hands. We raised our hands together before God.

I lodged with the pastor and his wife while I worked at this mission. When the pastor's wife had to go away from home, I returned to the home of Pastor Simon and Eunice.

It was 2006 and I had made ten trips to Africa. This visit to Africa was all about the orphanage. Much time was spent in discussion with Pastor Simon about it and, together, we drew up plans concerning what needed to be finished and calculated the amount of money needed to cover operational costs on a monthly basis. The orphanage was alive and operating, yet many details needed to be completed. The roofing was added so the orphanage was more secure. God's hand was active in this home for children.

We were planning to have an educational component at the orphanage. The children who lived there, and the children who visited the feeding centre, needed some structured activities. In the beginning, groups of children were gathered together for lessons. These groups were organized in various locations within the orphanage.

Pastor Simon and I created plans for a school. Teaching was initiated and specific areas were designated as classrooms. Pastor Simon and Eunice were both qualified teachers.

Pastor Simon had forfeited a very good teaching position with the school board in Nairobi in order to work with the children from the street. In 2006, Eunice was working as a teacher and principal of a teaching mission. She gave up her well-paid position to work at the orphanage. Both Pastor Simon and

God of the Impossible

Eunice were making positive contributions to the children and the orphanage overall.

I left for Canada on July 18. Once home, I followed up with the pastor at Christian Life Assembly. Prior to my trip to Africa, the pastor had indicated an interest in the orphanage. He had read my prayer letter and expressed a desire to help. Pastor Simon and I communicated regularly so that I could maintain a pulse on what was happening at the orphanage.

The interest shown by Christian Life Assembly was most welcome. I described the orphanage and the support needed. I outlined the current status of the situation and some of the problems encountered along the way. I related that due to my age, I felt it was important to find a credible organization to take over the orphanage.

The Christian Life Assembly in Winnipeg began communications with the Pentecostal Mission in Africa. Arrangements needed to be made in order that mission representatives from Canada could visit the orphanage. The visitation needed to include an assessment of the current status of the orphanage, and the creation of a plan for future developments. As well, administrative regulations needed to be formulated and contact personnel organized.

Donations for the orphanage would be provided to Pastor Simon directly from the Christian Life Assembly. Pastor Simon would be required to give account of all spending to the Pentecostal Mission in Africa.

Twelve

Outreach at Home

My outreach work in Winnipeg kept me busy on a daily basis. I visited Union Gospel Mission three times per week. There, I participated in worship, prayer and various volunteer activities. Later in the year, I spent more of my time at the Family Life Centre, which is a division of the Union Gospel Mission. The Family Life Centre provided programs that focussed on the spiritual needs of women in the community.

Two mornings per week, I visited the Vineyard Church and Drop-In Centre on Main Street. There, I shared the gospel and witnessed to the people. God gave me many verses, poems and scriptures. He gave me pictures to draw or paint and I prepared booklets containing these verses and pictures, then distributed them when I visited either the Union Gospel Mission or the Vineyard.

I felt an urgency to make every moment count for the Lord. I was transported by the Handy-Transit service to the various locations where I conducted my outreach service, and engaged in conversation with the drivers. Sometimes, I brought food along to give to the drivers who were often kept so busy that they did not take time for a meal. I used the time in the car as an opportunity to witness to them. Praise God! He was there to help me witness to people of other faiths. Some of these drivers gave their hearts to Jesus Christ.

The drivers often asked me what church I attended. I responded that I attended several churches but any church that I attended had to teach that Jesus is the way, and the Bible had to be the source of all teaching.

Singing and music has always been a special part of my life. I was asked to join the church choir when I was 12 years old. Throughout the years, I have used singing to brighten my days and uplift my spirit. Through the trials and tribulations of life, I have turned to music. I played the organ and later, the omnichord. Through the years, God has blessed me with a strong voice. My voice was an instrument that I could carry with me no matter where I travelled. Many people have known me to burst into song in their presence.

Over the years, God has also blessed me with many songs. One song in particular, *Channels Only*, has remained very precious to me. We are channels of God's love. I often think about how we are like a hose. This hose must be clean of sin so that we may channel God's love. *Channels of Love* has been such a blessing to me.

It has been my observation that when people receive goods that they need to survive in the world—food and clothing etc. — they receive something that is finite. The goods are used up and are gone. Many times, people have responded to the goods given to them in a selfish and wasteful manner. In contrast, when they receive God's love, the impact is infinite. They depart with something that moves them on the inside, something that endures.

I visit the Prayer Furnace, located on the eastern side of Winnipeg, four times per week, where people participate in Bible reading and intercessory prayer. The Prayer Furnace is a place where people can pray at any time. Prayer has continued consistently, twenty-four hours a day, seven days a week, since its conception. Prayer requests have been forwarded to the Prayer Furnace from all parts of the world. The walls are covered with these requests. The intercessors are guided by the Holy Spirit to pray for those who had their needs displayed on the wall. Many people from other lands have been persecuted for their faith. The intercessors have prayed for these individuals and their loved ones who remain after the people have died for their faith in Jesus Christ.

One of my visits to the Prayer Furnace was coupled with a weekly evening meeting held by The End Time Handmaidens and Servants. This group participated in praise and worship, intercessory prayer, and aimed to encourage others to live for God.

Over the last two years, people have been sharing with me, that in Winnipeg, there are groups available to address the needs of women. Similarly, there are groups in the community to assist men. However, programs for couples who need prayer are lacking.

Couples need instruction on how to use the word to develop a Godly home and raise their families according to the laws outlined in the Bible. In response, I meet with couples at the Prayer Furnace on Wednesday evenings. God makes a way for all of our needs, both as individuals and as groups of people.

What I am discovering is that individuals are not spending enough time in the word. Reading the Bible is very important so that we are aware of God's direction for our lives. The Bible is our instruction book and is as applicable to our lives today as it ever was.

There is a prayer furnace in Ottawa, Ontario, as well. Its close proximity to the federal government allows the intercessors to be cognizant of the agenda being brought forward in parliament. The intercessors are able to keep a pulse on changes that occur in the government and are able to relate those issues to other prayer furnaces across our nation. As well, there is a group of people in Ottawa who pray for our nation every morning. These individuals know that God is watching to see whether our nation is operating according to His word and His plans for the people in our country.

Canada is a wonderful country and we must remember to hold it up in prayer before our Lord so that we can continue to enjoy His blessings.

I have travelled quite extensively in the world. No matter where I have travelled there is no place like Canada. People in Canada have become complacent about their country.

I have also participated in Billy Graham Telephone Ministry on a regular basis every three months over the last five or six years. It responds to callers who have watched a spiritual message on television. The people who answer the phones take prayer requests and pass them on to prayer intercessors, such as myself. Together, and individually, we pray for those who have called the television ministry.

If someone phones who is contemplating suicide, the intercessors are notified immediately and engage in prayer for that soul. Many individuals have been saved from a tragic ending by the spiritual response of God to the prayers of those intercessors.

I have found my involvement in the Billy Graham Telephone Ministry to be both rewarding and uplifting. I have invited many others to become involved in this ministry. They began by taking the training provided by BGM. Many individuals have found a way to contribute to this ministry and have identified their God-given gifts.

I invited Mr. Graves to participate in the ministry and the very first time, he responded to several German-speaking callers. He was able to respond to their spiritual needs in their native tongue. We were struck by God's way of directing phone calls and making a way for the gospel to be shared.

Thirteen

Moving Forward

At the onset of another year, I sought the direction of the Lord through prayer. I needed to know His will for my life in the coming months. I was instructed to return to Africa on July 14. God wanted me to remain there until August 8. He directed me to be back in Canada in time for the International Conference of the End Time Handmaidens and Servants. The conference was scheduled to be held in Winnipeg.

I was contacted by a sister in the Lord who expressed her desire to accompany me to Africa. Later, her husband and son both decided to make the journey as well. In order to participate on a mission, one is required to complete an application. These individuals did not complete their applications fully, which alerted me to check with the Lord about the appropriateness of their visit to the orphanage. The Lord assured me that they should travel with me. I rested in the Lord knowing that we needed extra help at the orphanage.

Prior to our trip to Africa, a torrential rainstorm had moved through the Kibera slums. The supporting wall of the orphanage incurred a great deal of damage. In order to resurrect the wall fully, much physical labour would be required. One of the individuals, who planned to travel to the orphanage with me was knowledgeable and experienced in the construction industry. The father, with the help of his son and a hired man, rebuilt the wall, made repairs, constructed and refinished walls and ceilings. In addition, a new kitchen was built.

Everyone was able to offer a skill or help in some way. The mother painted flowers on the walls and gave the area a decorative appeal. The finishing touches made to the orphanage brought the environment alive.

The son brought his guitar to Africa and the children enjoyed his charismatic style of entertaining. I taught the children many songs and Eunice and I prepared the children for the production of a CD. It was our intention to record the voices of an African children's choir.

Following a whole afternoon of taping and singing, we learned that the taping was ineffective. Pastor Simon and I were very disappointed that the production of the CD was not successful. We were hopeful that we could sell CDs of the children's choir and, in turn, raise funds for the orphanage. All in all, it was a learning experience. We were grateful that the children had spent time singing their praises to the Lord. We knew in our hearts that God was an attentive audience.

On our final day in Africa, we went shopping to purchase trees and plants for the orphanage. Soil was brought in and put along the front wall where the gate is located. We planted fruit trees and many plants to border and frame the orphanage. God's home for the children was given a physical hedge of protection as well as a spiritual one.

By August 8, I was back in Winnipeg where I received an email from Pastor Simon. He said he would like to attend the End Time Handmaidens and Servants Conference. I thought that it would be beneficial for him to attend so I forwarded half of the money needed to purchase an airline ticket and instructed him to generate sufficient funds for the remainder of the cost. I directed him to consult with the management team in Africa.

Pastor Simon bought his airplane ticket and arrived in Winnipeg the day before the conference was scheduled to begin. He enjoyed the conference thoroughly and made many contacts, compiling a list of addresses and emails for future contact and consideration.

During the conference, Pastor Simon and I were invited to the stage to share about the work we were doing in the orphanage and the street ministry in Nairobi. I described the progress made at the orphanage and communicated that I had undertaken personal debt in order to cover the repairs and improvements necessary. As I continued sharing, people began to approach the stage. One by one, they came forward and laid money at my feet to pay the debt.

Praise God! He makes a way for my provision. He is my helper in my time of need.

The conference concluded and people made their way back to their homes. Pastor Simon approached me and asked for funds to pay for his return ticket to Africa. I reminded him of our initial agreement and informed him that the money received at the conference was provided for the debt I had incurred due to the construction done at the orphanage. I prayed earnestly about this situation because something did not seem right about it. I felt in my spirit that I should deny his request.

For confirmation, I consulted with the director of the End Time Handmaidens and Servants and was cautioned clearly and emphatically. The money was not given to pay for Pastor Simon's airfare back to Africa. I followed God's leading and applied all funds towards the debt at the orphanage.

Pastor Simon returned to Africa but even after the contributions made at the conference, I continued to have debt and cried out to God: "I did what I felt you wanted me to do. No more. No less. I need you to help me pay off this debt."

Shortly after my conversation with God, the buzzer rang in my apartment to alert me to the fact that someone was waiting to come for a visit. The voice on the other end of the intercom was familiar. It was the businessman, Derek, who had helped me at other times in the past. He asked if he could come upstairs to see me. He arrived at my apartment door and I welcomed him in.

Without hesitation, he began. "Mrs. Peters, you have been an inspiration to me. You have been a blessing. God has spoken to me. I need to pay off your debt for you."

I looked at him with mist in my eyes. I knew that his visit was the hand of the Lord reaching out to me once more.

Derek reached into his suit pocket and withdrew his cheque book. He looked at me and asked how much money was outstanding. I told him an amount and he proceeded to make out the cheque. I was so grateful to God for answering my prayer and for lifting that heavy burden. It was a blessing to see that Derek was a joyful giver. He was giving from the right place— his heart! I thanked him once more.

As he stood at my door ready to leave, I said, "I can't repay you, but God will."

It was March in Canada, the middle of winter, and I was still unsure if I was going to Africa again. One morning, the Lord said, "Find your calendar and make your arrangements."

In previous years, I travelled to Africa, in August, following the Handmaidens and Servants conference. I stayed for two or three weeks. This time, when I conversed with Pastor Simon about travel arrangements, he said, "Two or three weeks? That is not enough. We want you to come for a longer time."

I altered my travel plans and arrived in Africa in June. I was scheduled to visit for four weeks. Upon my arrival, I was struck by the many changes. As a result of unrest in Nairobi, Pastor Simon's residence was in a different location. He and his family left their previous home for safety. Unfortunately, his former residence was burned by the rebels. His new home was located in a place that required an uphill journey along a very rocky road.

Our journey to the orphanage was also an uphill climb. When we departed, it was difficult to move forward on the rocky ground and our progress was slow due to our unsure footing. Pastor Simon and I rented a car for the duration of my visit.

Resources were limited and not readily available. The cost of supplies had risen sharply. There was an obvious change in the children. Formerly, I noted that they took the food and supplies offered to them for granted. This time, they were visibly more grateful than I had ever seen them before. They were quick to acknowledge others and responded to gestures made to help them.

The changes were not limited to the orphanage. Pastor Simon's church had been ransacked by the rebels. As a result, the people were required to bring their own chairs or seats to the church. Many attended and sat on the floor. Later, due to the number of people taking a place on the floor, the church designated a portion of the collection to rent chairs for the people to use during the service.

One day, late in the morning, the children started singing praises. Their song was about me. While I was home in Canada, they had created this song that they were singing. I promptly stopped their singing and redirected their praises to God. I told them that if it was not for God, I would not have been able to come to Africa, and shared stories with them about my early years.

My life started in Russia. It was in Russia, where we were very poor, that God showered me with His grace. It was by God's grace that my family was able to emigrate to Canada. Even in Canada, we endured many years of poverty, many trials and hardships and years of sickness.

I looked out at the children who were now silent and simply staring at me. They seemed to look at me in a different way after that time of sharing. Their perception of me as a rich Canadian became more grounded in the truth. I was not a rich Canadian coming to their aid but rather someone who had lived an impoverished life at another time in history. I understood their fears and their hardships.

During the uprising, many farmers had been killed. Rice and vegetables were in short supply. The shortages resulted in price increases. The demand for food was great but food staples were expensive.

Upon arrival at the orphanage, I was required to pay $1,300 for a debt incurred during my absence. In order to provide food for the children, the debt accumulated. God's timing was impeccable. If I had visited later in the summer, as was the original plan, the children would have gone without food. The line of credit would have been exceeded later in the season. I paid the funds necessary to clear the debt and was grateful that God is the perfect planner.

We drove to markets that were about an hour from the orphanage toward the city, where we could get the necessary food stuffs and replenished supplies for the children. By God's grace, they would not go hungry.

We also purchased a huge water tank for the orphanage. The water supply was piped in from the city but only available during off hours when the more affluent people were not using the system. Initially, the water tank was installed with plastic pipes due to the prohibitive cost of copper piping. Later, the city threatened to discontinue our water supply because the pipes were leaking. The plastic pipes were replaced with copper ones and the leaking problem was resolved.

In the meantime, the water had caused damage to the cement floors, making them soft. The traffic of 100 people on a daily basis contributed to their destruction. They were replaced once more before I returned to Canada.

A highlight of my twelfth trip to Africa was the time I was able to spend singing with the children. They loved to sing and were eager to learn all of my songs. Sadly, the taping of our choir was never returned to me. I have carried the singing voices of the children in my heart throughout time since that visit. I have found such joy in my memories of the children singing to the Lord.

The Lord began speaking to me about letting go of the orphanage. It was time to let another take charge of the responsibilities that I had been holding onto. Confirmation came one day when a trusted pastor asked to speak with me. He told me that he thought he had a word from the Lord for me.

"Will you receive the word that I have for you?" he asked me.

I said that I would receive the word, which was that it was time to pass the ministry onto someone younger. Thank you, God, for sending a messenger to me. The word that you are sending my way is a confirmation. I receive your word Lord, and I set myself ready to trust and obey.

Fourteen

My Christian Walk

After my return to Canada in 2008, I experienced hip and neck pain. I believe it was the result of my travels over the rocky terrain in Africa. My trip to Africa was a blessing because I now am certain that a younger missionary is needed. I have been encouraged to learn that my grandson, Jonathan and his wife, Megan, have made plans to visit Africa sometime in the near future. Much of my physical discomfort and pain has been eased by the knowledge of my grandson's interest in the ministry.

Jonathan and Megan have been blessed with musical gifts. They intend to make a CD of the children of the orphanage singing praises to God. I am confident that he and Megan will be richly blessed by their active participation and the visible joy and enthusiasm expressed by the children of the orphanage when they sing.

God wants us to sing His praises with a willing heart. I recall that I told the children they could leave if they did not want to sing. Not one child left. Rather, one child from the back row called out to me and said, "We love to sing with you."

When I left Africa, I was uncertain whether I would be able to return to that continent. I left that decision with God. As I look back on my experiences in that land of the hot sun, I revel in the wonderful events that took place during my time there. God taught me many lessons.

Some people have aspired to their retirement years as a time of slowing down and taking it easy. For me, my retirement years have been full of activity on behalf of the Lord. I have not retired from my work as an intercessor and evangelist. In Canada, I have been told by many young people that they could not keep pace with my schedule. I have often thought of the verse in Psalms that states that we shall be fruitful even in our old age.

I believe that God has called me to intercession. I serve at the Prayer Furnace in Winnipeg, where I take my place as an intercessor on behalf of the people. While I spend time there on Monday, Wednesday, Friday and Saturday, I pray for the churches. I recall here, 1 Chronicles 7:14, in which God tells us:

"If my people which are called by my name shall humble themselves, and pray and seek my face, and turn from their wicked ways then I will hear from heaven, forgive their sins and will heal their land" (1 Chronicles 7:14).

Our land is Canada. Our land really needs healing. It is up to the churches to humble themselves and turn from their wicked ways, just as it is states in Chronicles. We all must pray for Canada.

Obey and be blessed. Disobey, and the blessings will be withheld and the devil will see to the curses. Disobey, and we open the door for the devil to attack us. If we read Deuteronomy 28, we find that the blessings and curses are listed.

God is true to His promises. God shows me that disobedience is like an umbrella. The umbrella stands in the way and stops God's blessings from falling on me. As I look back on my life, I see how God has blessed me because I have been willing to step out in obedience to Him. I did not think that I would see age

50, and now I am 84 years old. I am going strong and finding life very fulfilling. I owe it all to God.

I minister at the Vineyard Church in Winnipeg. There, I met a middle-aged man who was suicidal. I spoke with him about God. I encouraged this man by reading from the word of God. I prayed to God to show this man that there is a purpose for his life, which came from the heart of God. When I looked up into this man's eyes, his face was transformed. I noted a glow. He expressed his gratitude for my prayers and words of encouragement. What could be more encouraging than moments such as these?

At the Union Gospel Mission, where I visit three times per week, I met a woman in her early thirties. She expressed her anger towards God. As it turned out, she was abused by her earthly father. I responded to her anger by telling her about the abuse that I had suffered as a young girl. From this place of shared understanding, I told her that I would one day stand before God. I would have to account for my attitude. In turn, whoever abused me would have to account for his actions. In the end, this woman gave her life to Christ. The look on her face expressed gratitude and replaced the anguish that earlier was etched there.

People ask me, "What keeps you going at your age?"

I tell them about moments that I have experienced in my life, moments such as the ones shared in this book, and I encourage them to seek out a relationship with the Lord. I tell them that I trust in my God and He knows who I am and what is in my heart.

On March 11, 2009, I celebrated my eighty-fourth birthday. I was surrounded by Christian friends. I was blessed with two birthday cakes and wonderful fellowship. I am so grateful to God.

Hardships and trials have been present along my journey but they were blessings in disguise. Every experience was a lesson that I was called upon to draw from at another time in my life. Those hardships have served me well in my ministry over the years. My experiences have allowed me to relate to so many people along my walk. I have been a motherly figure to many individuals. These relationships have been such a blessing to me and I am eternally grateful to God for them.

In Africa, many young people refer to me as "Mama Helena". In Winnipeg, many young people seek my counsel when I am doing outreach. Many of them refer to me as their Mom.

In closing, I refer to a verse that God gave me when I began the television program years ago:

Now the God of peace, that brought again from the dead our Lord Jesus, that great shepherd of the sheep, through the blood of the everlasting covenant. Make you perfect in every good work to do his will, working in you that which is well pleasing in his sight, through Jesus Christ; to whom be glory forever and ever. Amen (Hebrews 13:20,21).

I was led to understand that the resurrection power is ours to do the will of God.

If it is God's will for me to do something, even if I feel incapable, God will equip me to do His will. God showed me that we can take nothing to heaven but the people we encouraged along the way to get there.

God Bless You, and Amen!

In Conclusion

In closing, I took the opportunity to speak with individuals who have been associated with Helena Peters over the years. In their own words, the following is what they had to say about her.

John Rademaker and his wife, Violet, are mercy pastors at the Winnipeg Centre Vineyard Church. These are his words to describe Helena Peters, based on his association with her at the Vineyard:

> *"Helena is a wonderful woman of God. She embodies the reality of God's presence and miraculous manifestation of provision for her vision and ministry. Her sweet spirit is infectious. She carries a passion for the salvation of anyone unsaved. She is unashamed to proclaim Jesus at any moment. She truly represents the Biblical standard for apostle and carries it with humility. She is a great model of devotion to and love for Jesus. She commands much respect and appreciation for her presence at the Vineyard each week."*

Greg Stetski, director of the Union Gospel Rescue Mission in Winnipeg, told me he has known Helena Peters for more than twenty years. Greg described Helena in this way:

"Gospel is what she is all about. Her single focus is sharing the gospel. She likes to make things to give to people; booklets and posters, which convey scripture verses. She loves to sing at the drop-in. She has been a very faithful visitor on a regular basis. She has been helping at the mission for twenty years. She has a real heart for the people to come to know Jesus.

"When she visits the mission, she always attends the prayer times because she knows that prayer is our power. She has remained aware of the mission focus throughout the years. She has participated at the Family Life Centre, more recently, and years ago with her husband. When she has shared about her mission work in Africa, the women at the Family Life Centre have expressed their desire to assist Helena. They have supported her work by taking collections when she has visited there."

Ramona Lee of the Family Life Centre in Winnipeg shared that she had known Mrs. Peters only a short time. She said:

"I met Helena in March, 2009 at the Family Life Centre where she visits once each week. From my experience with Helena, it is clear that she has a real heart for prayer. She is very sensitive in that way. Not a lot of people have that gift—that relationship with the Lord. Even though Mrs. Peters is frail, she wants to be at the Family Life Centre. I am reminded of a scripture. 'Though our outward man perish, yet the inward man is renewed day by day' (2 Corinthians 4:16). In a word, Helena is amazing!"

In Conclusion

Pastor Ivan Blakney of the Christian Life Assembly Church shared these sentiments:

"Helena is greatly respected at CLA. She is talkative and the people love her. She is a model for others and she demonstrates such compassion for people."

The pastor told me the church is happy to announce a recent development concerning the orphanage in Nairobi. He reported the following:

"The Pentecostal Assemblies Missions of Canada have agreed to assume responsibility for the orphanage in Nairobi, Kenya, founded by Mrs. Helena Peters. The orphanage has just been accepted for Child Care-Plus, through the Emergency Relief Development Overseas and in this way, sponsorships for the children will be managed. Currently, biographies of the individual children at the orphanage are being collected to facilitate the sponsorship process. Funding for the children will be collected on a monthly basis. It is a wonderful development."

I contacted Jonathan Mutch, director of the Pegwatch Prayer Furnace. Jonathan was happy to provide information about his association with Helena Peters. He indicated that Helena contributes nine or more hours per week at the PPF. He had this to share about her:

"Helena's outlook and attitude stood out to us from the start. Many people would check the 24/7 calendar to see what time would work for them to come to the Prayer Furnace. We are always grateful for those who come, but Helena asked us what time would be most helpful for us. She wanted to come when it was most needed. Once we

let her know which times were the most challenging for us to cover, she then organized her schedule around those times.

"While some people were very private with their prayer times, Helena seemed always ready to share her times with others. She not only spread the word about the PPF, bringing in people to enable the non-stop operation, but also encouraged people as far away as her beloved Kenya about having a house of prayer.

"Transportation was not easy for Helena. She did not let the trouble or expense of Handi Transit hold her back from ministry. I well remember one call that she left on our answering machine. It was a classic, and I wish there was some way to properly record it. Helena was so excited about praying with her driver to receive the Lord. From my conversation with others, I realized that this was not an uncommon occurrence."

In conclusion, this scripture makes me think of Helena Peters:

"Go home to your friends, and tell them what great things the Lord has done for you, and how He has had compassion on you." (Mark 5:19 NKJV).

About the Author

On many occasions, I would suggest to Helena that someone should write about her walk with God and to my surprise, one day she turned to me and said,

"I want you to write my story."

I was born in Winnipeg, Manitoba and grew up in the country. Like Helena, my father was a farmer. After graduating from high school, I moved to Alberta where I completed an undergraduate degree, qualified to work as a speech language pathologist, and began my professional career. Although I have remained passionate about my professional work, it was always my heart's desire to write a book. The word says *"Delight thyself also in the Lord; and he shall give thee the desires of thine heart"* (Psalm 37:4).

143